Who Goes Where and Why?
An Overview and Analysis of Global
Educational Mobility

Who Goes Where and Why?

An Overview and Analysis of Global
Educational Mobility

BY CAROLINE MACREADY AND CLIVE TUCKER

Fifth in a series of Global Education Research Reports

INSTITUTE OF
INTERNATIONAL
EDUCATION

New York

IIE publications can be purchased at: www.iiebooks.org

The Institute of International Education
809 United Nations Plaza, New York, New York 10017

Library of Congress Cataloging-in-Publication Data

Macready, Caroline.
  Who goes where and why? : an overview and analysis of global educational mobility / by Caroline Macready and Clive Tucker.
      p. cm. — (Global education research reports ; 5)
  Includes bibliographical references.
  ISBN 978-0-87206-342-6 (alk. paper)
  1. Transnational education. 2. Student mobility. 3. Education and globalization. I. Tucker, Clive. II. Title.
  LC1095.M32 2011
  378'.016—dc22
                        2011010169

Series editors:
Daniel Obst, Deputy Vice President for International Partnerships, IIE
Sharon Witherell, Director of Public Affairs, IIE
Editorial Contributors: Rajika Bhandari, Raisa Belyavina, Patricia Chow, Shepherd Laughlin, Gulienne Rollins

Cover and text design: Pat Scully Design
Chart and Table design: Kathy McGilvery

TABLE OF CONTENTS

CHARTS, TABLES, AND FIGURES

Charts

Tables

Figures

FOREWORDS

By Allan E. Goodman

The number of students pursuing degrees and conducting research in a culture beyond their own now totals some 3.3 million students. While students have always sought to broaden their cultural and educational horizons by enrolling at the most prestigious educational institutions around the world, the complexity of global mobility substantially changed as the 21st century began. We have seen changes in terms of who is going where, and in the mix of host and sending countries. Most countries now consider global educational mobility and educational exchanges as critical components for sharing knowledge, building intellectual capital, and remaining competitive in a globalized world.

Governments, business leaders, and educators worldwide have a growing interest in documenting these student mobility trends as more students seek higher education opportunities in the global marketplace. They are increasingly aware that higher education must keep pace with the ever more rapid flow of ideas, technology, people, and information.

The Institute of International Education (IIE) has a long history of conducting research on critical developments in global education mobility. Each year, the Institute publishes the *Open Doors Report on International Educational Exchange,* releasing new statistics and analyses of international and U.S. student flows based on surveys of accredited U.S. higher education institutions. For the past decade, IIE has also examined student flows on a global basis through *Project Atlas*, convening counterparts in 21 countries to collaborate on collecting and sharing accurate student mobility data and examining the broader global implications of student migration.

This book documents the scale and range of global educational mobility over the past decade. It examines why students move, how they choose destinations, and the impact of national policies in a variety of hosting and sending countries across the world. The authors' analyses and conclusions aim to inform discussion and illustrate for governments and educators alike the physical flows of internationally mobile students across national borders.

The Institute values its partnership with the American Institute For Foreign Study (AIFS), and we would especially like to commend Sir Cyril Taylor, the founder and Chairman of AIFS, for proposing this timely and important research study.

Allan E. Goodman
President & CEO, Institute of International Education

BY SIR CYRIL TAYLOR

This report surveys all movements of young people from one country to another for all educational purposes. It shows how enthusiastic young people all across the globe are taking up study opportunities abroad. Some move while still at school. Others move later, to undertake a college or university program; for a period of research or teaching; for short courses to enhance career prospects; to learn a language; or simply to experience another country during the student phase of their lives. International students come to the U.S. for all these purposes under Exchange Visitor programs; this report includes a full survey of these students, based on statistics kindly provided by the U.S. Department of State.

Though it looks at other mobility too, much of this report focuses on university and college students. The years 2000-2008 saw tremendous growth in the numbers going into higher education, in their home countries and abroad. Recent figures suggest that the financial crisis at the end of the decade has not caused the decline in international mobility that many feared. This report sees reason to hope that growth will continue, if not as fast as before. Many factors—notably the continuing surge of the Asian economies and the demographic pattern of most Asian countries—should remain strong growth drivers for the foreseeable future.

But the report makes clear that we should expect some significant changes in student mobility patterns. The flow of international students has so far been primarily "East-West"—from developing countries to those countries in North America and Europe that have well-established education systems and institutions with worldwide reputations. But as the economic power of less traditional destination countries grows, they are investing heavily in their own education systems. China already has universities with a global reputation and India has declared its ambition to create institutions that will attract students and researchers from across the world. The U.S. remains the most popular destination for international students, but may continue to lose market share; while the UK and Australia, whose student visa regimes are becoming less welcoming, could see both numbers and market shares decline.

As competition for internationally mobile students intensifies, countries that make themselves less attractive to international students will inevitably find that they are losing ground. This report brings together in a new way what we know about how and why students choose international destinations, and about national policies that help and hinder mobility. It highlights, too, how little attention has been paid to non-tertiary student mobility. The success of the few countries that encourage it shows considerable unmet demand.

The first decade of this century has provided many examples of international misunderstanding and mistrust. The chance for young people to study in different countries and to meet and work with people from different national backgrounds and traditions is one of the best ways to create the bonds of friendship and mutual understanding. It has never been more important to encourage young people to become cultural ambassadors to other countries and from their own.

Sir Cyril Taylor GBE
Founder and Chairman of the American Institute For Foreign Study

Executive Summary

PART I: AN OVERVIEW OF GLOBAL EDUCATIONAL MOBILITY

Chapter 1

Chapter 1 explains that this study is about the physical flows of internationally mobile students across national borders. It aims to cover all mobility for educational purposes (not just mobility at tertiary level, though that level is by far the best documented), all regions of the world, and all major destination countries. As well as finding out the facts, this study hopes to cast some light on the following issues:

- Is the recent strong worldwide growth in international student mobility likely to continue?

- Which destination countries are likely to increase their share of the international student market and which could see their share diminish?

- Which origin countries and regions are most likely to increase their numbers of outgoing international students in the future?

Though only around 2 percent of the world student population is internationally mobile, the number of foreign students enrolled in tertiary education worldwide grew by 85 percent from 2000–07, keeping pace with rises in tertiary student populations. Students, educational institutions, national economies, and governments all have a big stake in international student mobility and want it to continue. The years up to 2008 saw strong growth, though student travelled to more diverse destinations, which were often within their own regions. Will that growth continue in the next few years? We identify four reasons for optimism and three for caution.

Chapter 1: Key findings

Will worldwide growth in international student mobility continue to be strong?

Reasons for optimism:

- The concentration of world population in developing countries with rising birth rates, an increasing demand for education in these countries, and limited domestic capacity to provide education;

- The development of the global economy and the associated emergence of China, India, and other Asian countries as major economic powers;

- The great importance students attach to being taught in English and other world languages; and
- The untapped growth potential of mobility below tertiary level.

Reasons for caution:

- Concerns over "brain drain" have driven sending countries to build up their own tertiary systems;
- The rapid growth in transnational education means students can get at least some international education benefits without leaving home; and
- Early signs from a few key countries (the U.S., Australia) that the bumper years of mobility growth ended in 2009/10.

Conclusions: (1) international student mobility is in good health and there is good potential for future growth, though some uncertainty exists about whether and when that growth will come through; (2) there are likely to be radical changes in the pattern of supply and demand, in the market share of the main current providers, and in the education they offer to international students.

Chapter 2

Chapter 2 reviews what is known about international mobility at tertiary level. It highlights problems with the data: first, some countries count only nonresidents as mobile, while others count all non-nationals including long-term residents; second, international organizations and most countries lack usable information on enrollments for less than a year. The chapter notes that, counting only longer-term enrollments in 207 countries, over 3.3 million tertiary students were enrolled outside their country of citizenship in 2008, 10.7 percent more than in 2007. It records which countries have the biggest shares of the world international student market; which have the highest proportions of international students in their tertiary system; which countries export the greatest numbers of students; regional shares of international student imports and exports; and changes over time. The chapter also discusses international students' study levels and fields of study by country. Finally, it looks at what is known about short-term mobility facts and trends, finding information only on mobility from the U.S. (using IIE's *Open Doors* as a source) and under the EU's Erasmus scheme.

Chapter 2: Points to note

- Students from OECD countries still tend to study mainly in other OECD countries, but students from all countries now choose from a wider range of destinations than they used to.
- More internationally mobile students now move within their regions of origin, and those who move beyond have distinct preferences between other regions.

- The host region of East Asia and the Pacific was the third largest in 2007, after Western Europe and North America, with 18 percent of internationally mobile students, a share which had increased 5 percent since 2000 at the expense of all other regions except Latin America and Central Asia.

- Among OECD member and partner countries, destinations that saw the biggest growth from 2000–08 were Russia (nearly 250 percent), the Czech Republic (over 400 percent), New Zealand (over 600 percent), and South Korea (over 1,000 percent). The destinations that saw the least were Belgium (9 percent), Turkey (15 percent), the United States (31 percent), Germany (31 percent), and Sweden (35 percent). Because growth averaged 85 percent, even those who lost market share ended the period with higher numbers.

- In 2008, China, India, and South Korea dominated the world list of sending countries, followed by Germany, Turkey, France, Russia, Japan, the United States, Malaysia, Morocco, Kazakhstan, Uzbekistan, Canada, and Italy, all exporting more than 40,000 long-term tertiary students. Another 26 countries exported more than 20,000.

- For some countries, internationalization efforts are strongly focused on particular study levels (Type A, Type B or Advanced Research programs) or study fields.

- France, Germany, and Spain each sent over 25,000 students to other EU or European Economic Area (EEA) countries under the Erasmus scheme in 2008/9.

Chapter 3

Chapter 3 reviews what is known about international mobility below and beyond the tertiary level. Very little is known; few countries report relevant statistics to international organizations. However, the chapter presents information on mobility at secondary school level into the U.S., into Australia, and between EU/EEA countries under the Comenius scheme; mobility at postsecondary non-tertiary level, including VET, into the UK and Australia; mobility of professors and other academic staff, researchers, and scholars into the U.S. and under the EU's Erasmus scheme; and mobility of school teachers into the U.S. and between EU/EEA countries (also under Comenius).

Chapter 3: Points to note

- The well-organized exchange schemes in the U.S. and EU and the experience of countries like Australia and the UK reveal considerable enthusiasm among young people for non-tertiary mobility opportunities, making this a potential growth area.

- Good quality vocational education and training (VET) programs can be very attractive to international students. In 2009, Australia had more international students in VET than in higher education.

Chapter 4

Chapter 4 looks at why students move and how they choose destinations.

The chapter identifies three important "push factors." The first is that students cannot find what they want at home, in terms of quantity, quality, or range. We consider which countries this applies to, using the UNESCO method of comparing recent growth in domestic and international tertiary enrollment and other evidence. The second is that young people wish to study abroad to broaden cultural and intellectual horizons and improve job prospects.

The third push factor is that some young people study abroad to position themselves for the next stage of education or work. This has not been much mentioned in other international studies, probably because the authors lacked data on non-tertiary mobility. Thanks to the U.S. Department of State, we had access to data for all U.S. Exchange Visitor categories, which showed that the countries ranking high for participation in the secondary school students' scheme also tended to rank high in the scheme for undergraduates. This association holds particularly true of Asian countries. Other commentators confirm that many South Korean and Vietnamese students enter U.S. secondary schools as a launch pad for entering a U.S. university. The same "positioning" phenomenon can be seen by comparing the top 20 countries of origin for undergraduate and graduate students in the U.S., and the top 20 countries of origin for graduate students and professors, teachers, researchers, and scholars in the United States. The same association is seen in the UK, where former international students often fill researcher and other academic posts.

This chapter also looks at "anti-push factors" that deter some young people who would benefit from study abroad. These include financial impediments and travel or visa difficulties, as well as personal or family constraints. Findings from the latest EUROSTUDENT survey report are quoted to show the major significance of financial impediments, and how both sending and receiving countries can help to reduce them.

The chapter then discusses 12 "pull factors" that may draw internationally mobile students to choose one country over another as their study destination. We note that different factors tip the scale for different individuals, but that some factors seem particularly important to students from certain countries. We look specifically at the significance of world university rankings; the motivations of Chinese students; the countries that focus on offering specialized opportunities; which countries now offer courses taught in English; which countries benefit from traditional links, migration routes, or diasporas; relative tuition fees and living costs; the value of offering internationally recognized qualifications; the appeal of short courses with low dropout rates; and ways in which national policies may make countries more attractive as destinations.

Chapter 4: Key findings

Determining who goes where and why is a complicated task. "Push factors" (including positioning for future study or work) encourage students to leave their own country to study. "Anti-push factors" deter many who could have benefited. "Pull factors" induce students to choose particular destinations.

Important pull factors:

- High-quality study opportunities;
- Specialized study opportunities;
- Courses offered in a language mobile students speak or want to learn;
- Traditional links and diasporas;
- Affordable cost;
- Internationally recognized qualifications;
- Good prospects of high returns;
- Post-study career opportunities in destination country;
- Good prospects of successful graduation within a predictable time;
- Effective marketing by destination country/institution;
- Home country support for going there to study; and
- Helpful visa arrangements, both for study and for work while studying.

Chapter 5

Chapter 5 considers in more detail the impact of national policies in 15 major host or sending countries, presenting key facts about their inward and outbound student mobility and brief descriptions of their internationalization policies. The countries featured are the U.S., Canada, Mexico, China, India, Japan, the United Kingdom, France, Germany, the Netherlands, Spain, Sweden, Australia, New Zealand, and South Africa. Much of the national information comes from *Student Mobility and the Internationalization of Higher Education: National Policies and Strategies from Six World Regions—A Project Atlas® Report* (Bhandari, Belyavina & Gutierrez, 2011).

In its concluding section, the chapter notes that countries that wish to attract international students and persuade their own students to study abroad need to align national policies with the motivations of potentially mobile students. However, the chapter recognizes that even the best national policies cannot achieve big change overnight. On the basis of good practice in the 15 countries, "helpful" and "unhelpful" national policies are identified.

Chapter 5: Key findings

The 15 countries offer a number of success stories and a few cautionary tales.

Policies helpful for increasing inward student mobility include:

- Ensuring that students can find in your country something that they cannot get at home, or not in the right quantity/quality or at the right level;
- Having effective arrangements to make students aware of what your country offers, to convince them that it is more attractive than their alternatives, and to give them all the practical information and help they require to access it;
- Keeping international students' tuition fees and maintenance costs modest, or offsetting them with other support;
- Ensuring that immigration and visa rules are student-friendly;
- Bearing in mind that education is a ladder: if internationally mobile students can get onto a lower rung they are more likely to progress to a higher rung within the same country; and
- Ensuring that international students in the country are well-looked-after and maintaining links with past international students through alumni networks.

Policies helpful for increasing outbound student mobility, long-term or short-term, include:

- Providing practical information on outbound opportunities and how to access them;
- Supporting outgoing students financially, with grants and scholarships or by giving them the same student support they would get at home; and
- Government support for international collaborative ventures.

Unhelpful policies (usually unintended) include:

- Overcharging international students;
- Failing to provide comprehensive care and support for them; and
- Having immigration and visa rules that fail to recognize international students' special circumstances or discriminate unreasonably against some groups of students.

PART II: U.S. COUNTRY STUDY

The U.S. country study (part II) focuses on inward educational mobility to the United States. Every noncitizen and nonresident who wishes to come to the country as an international student needs a nonimmigrant visa, either an Exchange Visitor (J-1) visa or a student visa. This country study draws on IIE's annual *Open Doors: Report on International Educational Exchange*, and on unpublished J-1 visa statistics from the U.S. Department of State for the years 2006–09.

Section A gives a brief summary of the relevant visa arrangements. Section B presents and discusses information on all incoming college and university students, their study levels and fields, and the top 20 sending countries by year and study level. Most of the information comes from *Open Doors 2010* and goes up to 2009/10—the year in which China overtook India to reach the top of the list of countries sending college and university students to the U.S., thanks to an increase of nearly 30 percent over 2008/9 numbers enrolled in 2008/9. Demand for tertiary places was strong over the period 2005/6 to 2008/9—new international student enrollments in tertiary programs increased by 40 percent—but growth slowed in 2009/10.

Section C considers the 11 categories and 4 subcategories of the Exchange Visitor Program that have been classified as education-related, in the following scheme groups: Au Pairs, Camp Counselors, Summer Work/Travelers, Secondary School Students, College and University Students (Undergraduate, Graduate and Non-degree), Professors and Teachers, Research Scholars, Short-term Scholars, Trainees, and Interns. The section points out that J-1 visa statistics for a given calendar year (e.g., 2009) refer to the numbers ending, rather than beginning, their programs in that year. Some schemes such as Summer Work/Traveler, Camp Counselor, and Short-term Scholar have a maximum stay of 4 or 6 months; people on these may well have started their programs in the same calendar year. Other schemes have maximum stays of 12 months, 18 months, two years, three years, five years, or as long as studies take to complete; people on these schemes could have made their mobility decisions some years before the year they appear in the statistics. The chapter analyzes numbers coming to America under the schemes collectively and separately, noting how the relative popularity of different schemes and the top sending regions and countries changed over the period from 2006–09.

U.S. country study: Key findings

- International students remain keen to come to the U.S. and take advantage of the many and varied educational opportunities the U.S. offers. In June 2010, there were nearly a million international students in the United States on Student, Trainee, or Exchange Visitor visas who were actively undertaking educational or training programs.

- In the three years from 2005/6 to 2008/9, new international student enrollments in higher education programs increased by 40 percent. Though

2009/10 figures show only limited growth, total enrollments reached a record 690,923. The top five places of origin were China, India, South Korea, Canada, and Taiwan. The leading places of origin vary according to academic level; India, for example, sends the most graduate students.

- Of the Exchange Visitors in 2009, 38 percent were Summer Work/Travelers; 11 percent Non-degree Students; 10 percent Secondary School Students; 10 percent Research Scholars; 7 percent Camp Counselors; 7 percent Short-term Scholars; 5 percent Interns; 5 percent Au Pairs; 3 percent Trainees; 2 percent Graduate Students; 1.5 percent Undergraduate Students; and 1 percent Professors or Teachers. (Tertiary students may be on Exchange Visitor rather than Student visas, but only if supported by scholarships or their home governments—unavoidably, these international students appear in our figures for "all college and university students" as well as in our Exchange Visitor figures.)

- In 2008, 330,185 Exchange Visitors completed education-related programs. Numbers plunged to 269,213 in 2009 as the global recession hit. The declines were mainly in the shorter, less obviously career-enhancing forms of visit, such as Summer Work/Travel (whose numbers fell by over 50,000); increases were reported for Non-degree students, Undergraduates, Graduates and Research Scholars. The top five sending countries in 2009 were China, Germany, Russia, the United Kingdom, and Brazil. Top sending countries vary by scheme.

- There have been some significant recent changes in the top sending regions and countries, both for all college and university students and for Exchange Visitors.

- Over the past five years numbers from Asia have risen. In 2009/10, China overtook India to top the sending table for international students enrolled in U.S. colleges and universities. In the sending table for Exchange Visitors, China moved from 4th in 2008 (behind Russia, Germany, and Brazil) to 1st in 2009, having topped the rankings for Undergraduates, Graduates, Non-degree Students, Research Scholars, Short-term Scholars, Professors, and Teachers and risen rapidly up the rankings as a sender of Secondary School Students, Summer Work/Travelers, and even Au Pairs. India was not only the second-biggest sender of college and university students, but also ranked 20th for visitors sent under Exchange Visitor arrangements (4th for Research Scholars, 5th for Trainees). South Korea was the third biggest sender of college and university students and ranked 9th for numbers sent under Exchange Visitor arrangements. Japan fell to 6th for college and university students in 2009/10, having sent lower numbers every year since 2005/6, but improved its position in the 2009 Exchange Visitor rankings to 12th (3rd for Research Scholars and Trainees). Taiwan overtook Japan to rank 5th for sending College and University Students, and also ranked 15th for Exchange

Visitors. Thailand ranked 8th for Exchange Visitors and 15th for College and University Students. Vietnam was 9th for College and University Students and also a keen sender of Graduate and Secondary School students under Exchange Visitor arrangements. Saudi Arabia rose three places to 7th for College and University Students.

- The four European countries that ranked among the top 20 senders of College and University Students in 2006/7 are still in the top 20 of 2009/10, but all except France have fallen in the rankings: Turkey is now 10th, Germany 12th, the United Kingdom 13th, and France 17th. However, Europe remains the top sending region for Exchange Visitors. In the top 20 table for 2009, Germany came 2nd, and was 1st for Au Pairs, Secondary School Students, Trainees, and Trainees and Interns combined. Russia was the 3rd largest sender, and the top sender for Summer Work/Travelers. The United Kingdom ranked 4th overall, and 1st for Camp Counselors and Trainees. France was 6th, Turkey 7th, Ukraine 10th. Several Central and Eastern European countries that used to send significant numbers under Exchange Visitor schemes—including Poland, Bulgaria, Romania, and Slovakia—no longer do so, having joined the European Union and found new opportunities there.

- From South America, Brazil was 14th in 2009/10 for sending college and university students and 5th in the Exchange Visitor rankings (2nd for Au Pairs and Secondary School Students), though it ranked 3rd until recently. Colombia currently stands 19th in both the College and University Students top 20 and the Exchange Visitors top 20; it ranks 4th for sending Au Pairs.

- From North America, Canada ranked 4th for sending College and University Students in 2009/10, but was not in the Exchange Visitors top 20, though it did come in 4th for Camp Counselors and Trainees. Mexico ranked 8th for College and University Students and 13th in the Exchange Visitors top 20 (4th for Professors/Teachers, 6th for Au Pairs).

- In Oceania, the only country to send significant numbers to the U.S. is Australia, ranked 14th in the Exchange Visitors top 20 (2nd for Camp Counselors).

- South Africa, the largest African sending country, did not make it into the top 20 for either Exchange Visitors or college and university students, but ranked 6th for Camp Counselors and 8th for Au Pairs.

Part I: An Overview of Global Mobility

Chapter 1
INTRODUCTION AND OVERVIEW

Scope of the study

This is a study of global mobility for educational purposes. Our aim has been to capture the physical flows of internationally mobile students across national borders. Where possible, we exclude students who are foreign nationals but are already living in the country where they study, though many statistical sources include these students. The study covers all regions of the world and all major destination countries.

International student mobility for tertiary education purposes is well documented. This study has also tried to cover mobility for other education-related purposes before or after the tertiary stage, for example when people move across national borders for secondary, postsecondary, and vocational education or as researchers, academics, or teachers. For convenience, this report refers to all movers for educational purposes as "international students." Unfortunately, information on non-tertiary mobility is scarce and rarely comparable from country to country. Only for one country (the United States) have we presented a full analysis of incoming mobility for all education purposes, thanks to the U.S. Department of State, which gave us access to raw data on Exchange Visitors. Our analysis is also informed by IIE's annual *Open Doors* data, which is supported by the U.S. Department of State's Bureau of Educational and Cultural Affairs.

We hope that our study will also cast some light on the following perennially interesting issues:

- Is the recent strong worldwide growth in international student mobility likely to continue?
- Which destination countries are likely to increase their share of the international student market and which could see their share diminish?
- Which origin countries and regions are most likely to increase their numbers of outgoing international students in the future?

Why is student mobility important?

The available information tells us that only a very small minority of the total world student population is internationally mobile—about 2 percent at tertiary level in 2007. This is only marginally higher than in 1999, when the figure was 1.9 percent. However, from 2000–07 the number of foreign students enrolled in tertiary education worldwide grew by 85 percent, thanks mainly to a very rapid rise in the world student population. The growth in tertiary numbers has occurred in almost every country and region of the world, but has been stronger in developing than in mature education systems. Chapter 2 of this report considers recent trends in the origins and destinations of tertiary students. Chapter 3 attempts a similar analysis of other, non-tertiary movements for educational purposes, although far less information is available on this category of students.

Up to 2008 (the latest year for most internationally comparable data), young people remained as keen to study abroad as ever, despite the growth of tertiary opportunities at home and the rapid development of different forms of "transnational education." As this report explains, international education meets a range of needs and demands. These can be seen from the perspective of at least three different groups: students, educational institutions, and national economies and governments.

The student perspective

The opportunity to study in another country is often decisive in shaping students' lives. They make a decision to spend substantial time abroad, often at considerable expense to themselves or their families, in order to acquire a foreign qualification, earn credit toward a domestic qualification, or take up an opportunity they see as not available locally. In chapter 4 we consider the available evidence about what motivates students to study abroad, what may hold them back, and which factors influence their choice of destination (country or host institution). One important motivating factor is a lack of suitable opportunities in the student's home country. Other reasons that students go abroad to study include a desire to enhance qualifications and employability back home, an intention to use study abroad as a path to work abroad, or a simple wish to experience another society and culture.

The perspective of host institutions

Most universities believe that the quality of the educational experience they offer is enriched by the presence of international students, at all levels from undergraduate studies to doctoral and postdoctoral research. Many institutions have longstanding scholarship or exchange programs that deliver a steady stream of students from other countries. Increasingly, however, universities and colleges value international students for economic reasons: the tuition fees paid by international students can be an important source of income, particularly at times of economic difficulty when other income sources are threatened. As a result, competition for international students becomes increasingly intense at both the national and institutional levels.

The perspective of national governments

The economic benefits of international student mobility are significant, if not necessarily distributed equally between countries that are net suppliers of students and those that are net receivers. For countries that attract large numbers of international students, the benefits are substantial: international students contributed $19.9 billion to the U.S. economy in 2009/10, according to the U.S. Department of Commerce. In the same year, the international activities of UK universities contributed £5.3 billion ($8.48 billion) to UK exports. For some countries, higher education is big business and a significant source of export income. As a result, some countries actively promote their universities and colleges internationally. Australia, for example, has invested large sums in marketing its higher and vocational education to other countries and has experienced a rapid growth in the number of international students it attracts. We examine the internationalization policies of governments, and their impact on international student mobility, in Chapter 5.

A future of continuing growth?

With this combination of stakeholders, it seems likely that international student mobility is here to stay. The world of learning and scholarship has often aspired to transcend national boundaries throughout history, and universities have traditionally been international institutions. But most levels of education now increasingly operate in an international market; universities, colleges, and institutes compete for students not only within their own country but also with their counterparts in other countries. As research institutions, universities are microcosms of the global economy; for example, one out of every three members of the research staff of the UK's Russell Group of leading research universities comes from outside the UK. The student populations of major universities also increasingly reflect the demands and opportunities of the global economy.

Can we therefore expect international student mobility to continue to increase at the rates seen in the last few years? This study offers four reasons for optimism and three reasons for caution.

The first reason for optimism is that world population growth is largely concentrated in developing countries with rising birth rates, and hence an increasing demand for education at all levels. It is true that China—currently the top supplier of mobile students—is expected to experience a decline in its population of 15- to 19-year-olds, from 117 million in 2005 to 85 million in 2020, as a result of the one-child policy; additionally, the Chinese higher education system has seen huge expansion over the last decade. Despite these factors, many students in China each year cannot find places at leading Chinese institutions, and many of these students possess the wealth and drive to study overseas. Twenty percent of China's 1.3 billion people are 14 or younger, which represents a potential pool of 260 million college students over the medium to long term. In India, the population of 15- to 19-year-olds was 114 million in 2005, and is expected to rise to 127 million by 2020. Other countries with large populations, such as Indonesia with 237 million, have very low numbers of mobile students (Indonesia had 36,800 in 2008, according to OECD/UNESCO), and hence a huge potential for growth. By contrast, many of the countries that are currently the main tertiary education destinations for international students have aging populations and static or declining birth rates, and hence a declining demand for education. This coincidence of expanding demand and available supply should sustain the overall growth of international student mobility, at least in the short to medium term.

The second reason for optimism is the development of the global economy and the associated emergence of China, India, and other Asian countries as major economic powers, strongly reinforcing the demand for international education. What is less clear is the likely impact on longstanding major destination countries, such as the U.S. and the UK, as these new economic powers increase the quantity, range, and quality of domestic study opportunities (and increasingly attract overseas students of their own). The attraction of studying at one of the world's highest-ranking universities in North America or Europe will remain very powerful for students who have the financial resources to study abroad and who aspire to a career in international business, but less affluent students—a likely source of further growth—will increasingly consider other destinations in an attempt to balance quality, cost, and accessibility. Applications from Indian students to study in the U.S. are already dropping off as India's potentially mobile students begin to consider a wider range of options, both at home and abroad. Recently, mobile students have increasingly studied abroad within their own regions, and this trend is likely to continue.

A third reason for optimism, highlighted by our analysis in chapter 4 of the motives for international student mobility, is the continuing importance of such factors as language. The English language may be only one of several "world languages"—perhaps behind Mandarin and Spanish in terms of number of native speakers—but it is the working language of the global economy. Twenty-three percent of internationally mobile students are studying business and administration. Young people who expect to pursue global careers understand the importance of being able to work in English. The attraction of studying in the English language in a major city in an English-speaking country at an institution with a worldwide reputation is significant. It should be no surprise, therefore, that English-speaking countries account for nearly 45 percent of all international student places (chapter 2). Chapter 4 also highlights the growth of English-language courses in non-English-speaking countries, particularly in Continental Europe but also in countries such as China, Japan, and South Korea. There is also growing interest in studying Chinese for at least part of a tertiary course. We expect ambitious young people to remain interested in studying abroad partly because of the career advantages of learning to work in another language.

A fourth reason for optimism is that, although it is difficult or impossible to estimate non-tertiary educational mobility in most countries, available evidence suggests that such mobility is more extensive than normally assumed and possesses significant growth potential. As pointed out in chapter 4, one important reason why people study abroad is to position themselves for the next stage of their lives, which may be education or work. Our U.S. country study in part II, which examines incoming mobility under a range of education-related U.S. Exchange Visitor programs, picks up clear signs both of mobility during secondary education to improve tertiary opportunities and of mobility for first degrees to improve access to higher degrees and academic posts. Countries that encourage mobility or short-term student visits at lower educational levels may well reap longer-term economic benefits as they attract more tertiary-level students. Also, some countries have found rich rewards in developing internationally attractive programs in areas like vocational education and training (VET). Australia, for example, has been very successful in attracting international students into higher education, where numbers grew by 25 percent from 2005–09; but meanwhile, the numbers of international students enrolled in VET grew by over 250 percent, until VET enrollments exceeded higher education enrollments. In the UK at present, half of all non-EU student visas are for study below degree level.

These are powerful reasons to expect current trends to continue, but other factors could exert a countervailing pressure.

The first reason for caution is that international student mobility is not always an unequivocal good for countries of origin. For these net exporting countries, many of which are in the developing world, the benefit of the skills and qualifications gained from returning students has to be set against the "brain drain" of those who do not return but instead pursue careers in the (predominantly developed) countries where they study. Few countries seem to put any obstacles in the way of their students who want to study abroad, and even where they do, it is not clear that they are motivated solely by fear of losing skills (chapter 4). But some of the countries that are leading suppliers of international students have a strong incentive—and, increasingly, sufficient economic resources—to create their own world-class universities. The Indian Institutes of Technology are one example; a number of other countries, such as Kazakhstan, are trying to create similar institutions. Both India and China have set themselves the objective of building world-class higher education sectors that will be attractive to students from all countries. The logic of globalization and the continuing strength of their economic growth suggest that they will succeed: the China Europe International Business School MBA program reports a 153 percent increase in the number of applicants over the last five years (Hanbury-Tenison, 2010).

A second reason for caution is that the rapid growth in various forms of transnational education (TNE) is making it possible for students to gain at least some of the perceived advantages of international study without the expense of leaving their own country. In 2008/9, there were 369,000 international students enrolled in UK higher education institutions, but a further 388,000 students were studying for a UK qualification outside the UK. In 2009, there were 162 UK higher education campuses operating globally in 51 countries, an increase of 43 percent over 2006. So far the demand for higher education in Asia has been so strong that TNE growth has not had any measurable impact on student mobility. Studying in another country, especially an English-speaking one, has attractions for young people seeking to equip themselves for global careers that TNE cannot offer. But some less prestigious universities may find it progressively harder to compete for international students when courses and qualifications comparable to theirs can be delivered around the world through shared courses leading to joint degrees and other credentials.

A third, and serious, reason for caution is that the impact of the 2009 global recession has yet to show up in internationally comparable student mobility data (the latest data from UNESCO and OECD is for 2008). Later figures now coming through from individual countries suggest that growth rates are slowing down, or even falling in some countries and at some levels. In the U.S., data from IIE's *Open Doors 2010* show that in 2009/10 international tertiary enrollments rose by only 2.9 percent, following increases of 7 percent or more in the previous two years; five of the top 10 sending countries had fewer tertiary students enrolled than in 2008/9; and new enrollments in undergraduate and graduate degree courses actually fell. Also, 2009 saw big drops in numbers of educational exchange visitors to the U.S. on some short-term programs. And in Australia, total enrollments of international students declined by 1.6 percent in January–November 2010 compared with the same period in 2009, mainly due to steep drops in numbers in English-language classes. Tertiary institutions predict that lower English-language class enrollment will cause under-graduate enrollments to decline in 2012. It is too early to say whether these "straws in the wind" signify the start of a general downward trend in international student numbers, a global blip that will be followed by general recovery, or just a problem (temporary or lasting) for a few leading destination countries.

A changing pattern of supply and demand?

Finally, what changes are likely in the future pattern of international supply and demand? Will the countries and regions that currently provide the most international students and those that currently offer them the most places remain the same? As we have indicated above, there are good reasons to expect that many current trends will be maintained. But, whether or not the volume of international student mobility continues to grow, it seems reasonable to assume that the pattern of supply and demand will become richer and more complex.

For both demographic and economic reasons, as noted above, the rapidly developing countries of Asia are likely to remain the main source of growth in the number of international students. Some large developing countries—notably Indonesia—have a significant capacity for growth in international student numbers that has hardly begun to be tapped. And, as we have noted, more and more young people from Asia have the financial resources and motivation to study abroad. Another region increasing in economic importance and with untapped student growth capacity is South America.

Where will the "new" internationally mobile students go? Today's leading host countries, with their world-class institutions, range, and diversity of courses and internationally recognized qualifications, will no doubt continue to exert a strong attraction, especially if they also offer the opportunity to master the English language. But it seems likely that their share will continue to decline. Study costs in the traditional destinations will seem extremely high to the emerging middle class in many countries. Increasingly, students will be able to find attractive alternatives, less costly and of acceptable quality, through transnational education or within their region. Many countries and regions in the developing world are investing in education centers that may soon become prestigious and desirable to students in neighboring countries. China and India are consciously building up their universities to be international institutions, and Singapore aims to become an educational hub for Southeast Asia. All these factors suggest that mobile students will increasingly choose destinations within their own regions. Meanwhile, the logic of globalization suggests that more and more mobile students from the developed world, who have traditionally studied largely in other developed countries, will see career advantages in studying in the developing world, particularly in countries such as China, which already possesses educational institutions known around the world.

There are also likely to be some changes in market share within the group of leading host countries. One potent cause of change is developments in immigration policy. Australia, a country that in the past has invested considerable resources in attracting international students (with notable success), now expects that overseas student arrivals will decline by more than 50 percent between 2010 and 2014, following changes in student immigration rules (see chapter 5). In the UK, the government is proposing radical cuts in the number of student visas. These cuts will be directed mainly at students seeking courses below degree level (although not at school level), but since about one-third of international students pursuing degree courses in the UK have previously studied in the UK (at language or further education colleges) the effect of the restrictions seems likely to be felt at all levels, including higher education. Other countries that offer courses in English at world-class institutions can, of course, be expected to accept more international students to compensate for reduced enrollments in countries such as Australia and the UK.

Conclusions

To sum up, international student mobility is in good health and there is good potential for future growth, but there are also reasons to be cautious about predicting whether and when that growth will come through. Such growth is likely to evolve in ways that bring radical changes in the pattern of supply and demand, in the market share of the main current providers, and in the education they offer to international students.

Chapter 2

GLOBAL STUDENT MOBILITY IN TERTIARY EDUCATION

Introduction

Many challenges complicate the task of comparing international student mobility figures from different countries. The first major problem is that there are three different ways of defining and counting international students: 1) all foreign nationals regardless of whether they already live in the country; 2) all non-citizens and/or permanent residents of the country; and 3) all those whose prior education—in the case of tertiary students, their secondary education—was in another country. In 2005, OECD and UNESCO revised their preferred basis for student mobility reporting from method 1 to method 2 or, if this suits countries' circumstances better, method 3. OECD and UNESCO call students counted by methods 2 or 3 "international students" and those counted by method 1 "foreign students" (OECD, 2010, p. 311-312). We will do likewise, referring to "overseas students" when discussing both together.

The second problem is that different countries tally their figures for international or foreign students on different time bases, often depending on whether the primary purpose of collecting the figures relates to education, immigration, or internationalization. Official statistics may count and report international/foreign students on the basis of when they get their visas, when they enroll in their educational institution, whether they are enrolled at the spot date in the year when the count takes place or when they complete their courses. In this chapter, we intend to use the best available figures, while including suitable warnings about mixing and matching non-comparable figures.

The scale of global mobility

In the 2010 edition of *Education at a Glance*—on which we draw heavily in the next few paragraphs—OECD reports that in 2008, over 3.3 million tertiary students were enrolled outside their country of citizenship. This represented a 10.7 percent increase from 2007 in total foreign student intake reported to the OECD and the UNESCO

Institute for Statistics, which cover 207 countries between them. The number of foreign tertiary students enrolled worldwide has increased by 85 percent since the year 2000. However, as UNESCO's *Global Education Digest 2009* notes, the percentage of tertiary students leaving their home countries to study has remained stable, at about 2 percent, since 1999. Overall, the recent rise in student mobility has simply kept pace with the worldwide growth in tertiary enrollment over the same period.

It should be noted that OECD and UNESCO figures exclude students enrolled in courses lasting less than a year. If students going overseas for any part of their tertiary education were included, the figures would be significantly higher. Many tertiary students, particularly from the U.S. and Europe, study abroad for a semester, a term, or just a few weeks under exchange or partnership arrangements between universities. We will consider what is known about shorter-term mobility in tertiary education later in this chapter.

Where do international students go?

In 2008, half of all foreign students went to just five countries. The United States received 19 percent; the United Kingdom 10 percent; and Germany, France, and Australia received 7 percent each. As chart 2.1 shows, the next five most popular destinations were Canada, Russia, Japan, Italy, and Spain. Places 11–20 were taken by

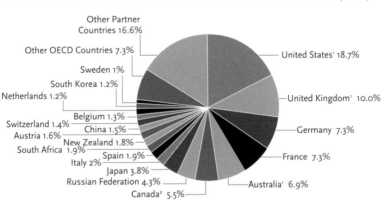

CHART 2.1: FOREIGN STUDENTS IN TERTIARY EDUCATION, BY DESTINATION COUNTRY (2008)

Other Partner Countries 16.6%
Other OECD Countries 7.3%
Sweden 1%
South Korea 1.2%
Netherlands 1.2%
Switzerland 1.4%
Austria 1.6%
South Africa 1.9%
Belgium 1.3%
China 1.5%
New Zealand 1.8%
Spain 1.9%
Italy 2%
Japan 3.8%
Russian Federation 4.3%
Canada[2] 5.5%
United States[1] 18.7%
United Kingdom[1] 10.0%
Germany 7.3%
France 7.3%
Australia[1] 6.9%

1. *For United States, United Kingdom, and Australia, data relate to international students rather than foreign students.*

2. *Canada's figures are for 2007 rather than 2008.*

Source: Reprinted from UNESCO Institute for Statistics (2010). Global education digest 2010: Comparing education statistics across the world. Montreal: UNESCO-UIS. (www.uis.unesco.org).

South Africa, New Zealand, Austria, China, Switzerland, Belgium, the Netherlands, South Korea, Sweden, and the Czech Republic.

As a result of these movements, some countries' tertiary systems have a very substantial proportion of students who have travelled from another country for study purposes. Chart 2.2 shows international students as a proportion of all tertiary enrollments. The list is led by Australia, where over 20 percent of tertiary students are international students, followed in this order by Austria, the United Kingdom, Switzerland, and New Zealand, all with over 10 percent of tertiary students from another country. Belgium, Canada, and Sweden have more than 5 percent.

Not shown in chart 2.2 are some popular destination countries that do not keep figures for non-citizen international students, but only for non-national foreign students; foreign student figures tend to be higher than international student figures because "foreigners" may include a number of long-term residents. Such countries include France, with foreign students accounting for 11.2 percent of tertiary enrollments, and Germany, with 10.9 percent.

CHART 2.2: STUDENT MOBILITY IN TERTIARY EDUCATION (2008)

Percentage of international students in tertiary enrollments

Student mobility – i.e. international students who travelled to a country different from their own for the purpose of tertiary study – ranges from below 1% to more than 20% of tertiary enrollments. International students are most numerous in tertiary enrollments in Australia, Austria, New Zealand, Switzerland, and the United Kingdom.

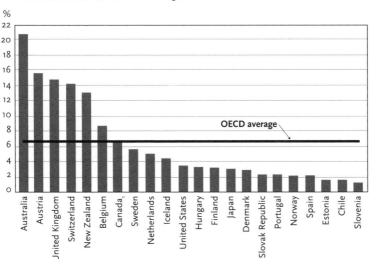

Note: The data presented in this chart are not comparable with data on foreign students in tertiary education presented in pre-2006 editions of Education at a Glance or elsewhere in this chapter.
1. Year of reference 2007.
Countries are ranked in descending order of the percentage of international students in tertiary education.
Source: OECD. Table C2.1. See Annex 3 for notes (www.oecd.org/edu/eag2010)

Different countries' shares of the global market for mobile tertiary students—shown in chart 2.1 for 2008—have changed quite a bit in the last decade. Chart 2.3 illustrates these changes.

As chart 2.3 shows, from 2000–08 the biggest loser was the United States, which saw its market share drop from 26 percent to 19 percent. Germany, the UK, Belgium, France, South Africa, and Sweden also lost market share. Notable gainers were Australia, Russia, New Zealand, and South Korea. However, due to the 85 percent increase in global tertiary student mobility from 2000–08, every OECD country and partner country saw its absolute numbers of foreign or international students grow (OECD, 2010, table C2.1).

CHART 2.3: TRENDS IN INTERNATIONAL EDUCATION MARKET SHARES (2000, 2008)

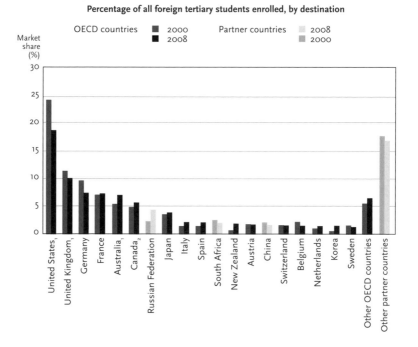

Percentage of all foreign tertiary students enrolled, by destination

1. Data relate to international students defined on the basis of their country of residence.

2. Year of reference 2007.

Countries are ranked in descending order of 2008 market shares.

Source: OECD and UNESCO Institute for Statistics for most data on partner countries. Table C2.7, available on line. See Annex 3 for notes (www.oecd.org/edu/eag2010).

TABLE 2.1: FOREIGN STUDENTS ENROLLED IN TERTIARY EDUCATION, BY COUNTRY AND REGION OF ORIGIN (2008)

Country	Numbers	Country	Numbers	Region	Numbers
1. China	510,842	22. Hong Kong	34,970		
2. India	184,801	23. Greece	34,196	Asia	1,653,738
3. South Korea	115,464	24. Pakistan	32,903		
4. Germany	94,408	25. United Kingdom	28,712		
5. Turkey	65,459	26. Mexico	28,627	Europe	817,709
6. France	63,081	27. Romania	27,650		
7. Russia	58,983	28. Brazil	27,571		
8. Japan	52,849	29. Cyprus	27,360	Africa	396,684
9. United States	52,328	30. Slovakia	27,084		
10. Malaysia	51,434	31. Nigeria	27,057		
11. Morocco	50,885	32. Bulgaria	26,044	South America	228,835
12. Kazakhstan	47,644	33. Thailand	25,944		
13. Uzbekistan	47,215	34. Spain	24,983		
14. Canada	45,157	35. Bosnia & Herzegovina	24,175	North America	99,123
15. Italy	42,443	36. Saudi Arabia	24,646		
16. Iran	39,983	37. Belarus	23,790	Oceania	34,553
17. Poland	38,641	38. Colombia	23,306		
18. Ukraine	38,048	39. Albania	23,170		
19. Vietnam	37,991	40. Algeria	22,903		
20. Indonesia	36,786	41. Cameroon	20,317		
21. Zimbabwe	36,645			World	3,343,092

Source: OECD (2010). Education at a Glance 2010, Table C2.7.

Where do international students come from?

Table 2.1, again based on OECD figures (OECD, 2010, table C2.7), shows the main countries of origin (all countries sending 20,000 students or more) and regions of origin for foreign tertiary students coming to OECD and partner countries in 2008. Some of these countries have a long tradition of sending students abroad, while others have become major senders relatively recently.

Host / Origin	AS % (% +/-)	CEE % (% +/-)	CA % (% +/-)	EAP % (% +/-)	LAC % (% +/-)	NA % (% +/-)	WE % (% +/-)	SWA % (% +/-)	SSA % (% +/-)
Arab States (AS)	15.9 (+3.7)	5.6 (-2.8)	0.4 (-0.1)	4.7 (+3.5)	0.1 (0)	15.4 (-1.3)	56.9 (-3.1)	1.0 (+0.1)	0.0 (0)
Central & East Europe (CEE)	0.2 (-0.1)	27.7 (+2.9)	3.1 (+0.7)	1.2 (+0.1)	0.0 (0)	12.3 (-2.9)	55.4 (-0.7)	0.0 (0)	0.0 (0)
Central Asia (CA)	0.3 (+0.1)	44.2 (-16.2)	34.7 (+6.2)	3.2 (+2.4)	0.0 (0)	4.9 (+1.3)	12.5 (+6.4)	0.1 (-0.2)	0.0 (0)
East Asia & Pacific (EAP)	0.2 (-0.3)	1.3 (-0.4)	0.4 (+0.3)	41.8 (+6.0)	0.2 (+0.1)	33.0 (-10.0)	22.9 (+4.4)	0.2 (-0.1)	0.0 (0)
Latin America & Caribbean (LAC)	0.1 (0)	0.3 (0)	0.0 (0)	2.5 (+0.9)	22.9 (+12.2)	43.2 (-11.7)	30.9 (-1.4)	0.0 (0)	0.0 (0)
North America (NA)	0.4 (+0.1)	2.3 (+0.5)	0.1 (0)	15.4 (+6.4)	1.7 (-0.9)	39.1 (-0.6)	40.5 (-5.6)	0.5 (+0.1)	0.0 (0)
West Europe (WE)	0.6 (+0.4)	3.9 (-0.6)	0.0 (0)	3.7 (+1.0)	0.2 (+0.1)	14.4 (+0.1)	77.2 (-1.0)	0.0 (0)	0.0 (0)
South & West Asia (SWA)	0.8 (-0.4)	3.2 (-2.3)	1.8 (-0.1)	21.1 (+11.5)	0.0 (0)	45.7 (-5.2)	26.1 (-2.0)	1.3 (-1.4)	0.0 (-0.1)
Sub-Saharan Africa (SSA)	3.0 (-0.5)	0.9 (-0.2)	0.0 (0)	4.3 (+2.4)	0.9 (-0.7)	17.4 (-2.0)	49.8 (-2.3)	0.8 (-1.2)	22.9 (+4.5)
World Total	2.9 (-0.4)	7.1 (-0.1)	1.9 (+0.5)	18.4 (+5.0)	1.9 (+0.7)	23.7 (-3.2)	41.2 (-2.3)	0.4 (-0.1)	2.6 (0)

Source: Reprinted from UNESCO Institute for Statistics (2009). Global education digest 2009: Comparing education statistics across the world. Montreal: UNESCO-UIS. (www.uis.unesco.org).

Note: Like OECD, UNESCO prefers to define "mobile students" as those who study in a foreign country of which they are not a permanent resident; but some countries were unable to report their figures to UNESCO on this basis. Where countries did not supply figures for 1999 or 2007, the nearest available previous year was used. Despite the gaps and comparability problems, UNESCO believes that this data reflect current global patterns of cross-border student mobility.

Recent trends in origins and destinations

There are distinct patterns in mobility between countries and regions. OECD students enroll predominantly in other OECD countries. UNESCO's *Global Education Digest 2010* records that the most common destination countries for Chinese students were the U.S. and Japan. OECD also notes that mobile students now choose from a wider range of destination countries than they used to, and that more of them move within their regions of origin.

Table 2.2, based on UNESCO figures, shows the percentages of mobile students coming from and going to each region of the world in 2007, and how these percentages increased or decreased from 1999–2007 (figures inside brackets). By comparing figures in brackets in the shaded diagonal column (change in share of own region's international students) with figures in brackets in the bottom row (change in share of the world's international students), it can be seen that with one exception, South and West Asia, all regions' percentages of home-region students have grown more, or declined less, than their percentages of world students. This table represents relative shares, not absolute numbers. Regions shown as exporting or importing lower percentages of the world total of mobile students in 2007 than in 1999 may well be exporting or importing more mobile students than they used to; it is just that other regions' numbers have increased more.

In 2007, Western Europe was still the biggest host region, drawing 41 percent of internationally mobile students, though its share had declined since 1999. Of all internationally mobile students in Western Europe, 77 percent were from the region, though this figure had also fallen since 1999. Western Europeans going elsewhere were most likely to choose destinations in North America (14 percent), but since 1999 more have favored East Asia and the Pacific and the Arab States. Very few mobile students from Western Europe go to Central Asia, South and West Asia, or Latin America and the Caribbean.

North America was the next-biggest host region in 2007, with 24 percent of internationally mobile students, though its share had declined more than Western Europe's over the period since 1999. By a small margin, this region's students preferred Western European destinations (40.5 percent) to destinations within North America (39 percent), though Western Europe's popularity had fallen more since 1999. Of internationally mobile students from North America, 15 percent went to East Asia and the Pacific, 6 percent more than in 1999. Over the same period, North Americans increasingly went to Central and Eastern Europe, and were less likely to go to Latin America and the Caribbean. Very few mobile students from North America went to Central Asia, the Arab States, or South and West Asia.

East Asia and the Pacific was the third-biggest host region in 2007, with 18 percent of internationally mobile students, a share that had increased 5 percent over the period at the expense of all other regions except Latin America and the Caribbean and Central Asia. Students from this region went in the largest numbers to other countries within the region (42 percent), followed by North America (33 percent). This was a reversal of the 1999 positions, when 43 percent moved to North America and 36 percent moved within the region. Students from East Asia and the Pacific increasingly went to Western Europe (up 4 percent) and Central Asia, and were less likely to go to Central and Eastern Europe. Very few mobile students from this region went to the Arab States, South and West Asia, or Latin America and the Caribbean.

Central and Eastern Europe was the fourth-biggest host region in 2007, with 7 percent of the world's internationally mobile students, 36 percent of them going to Russia. Western Europe was the destination of 55 percent of the region's mobile students, while 28 percent moved within the region and 12 percent went to North America. Over the period from 1999–2007, CEE students became more likely to move within the region, to Central Asia, and to East Asia and the Pacific; they were less likely to go to North America or Western Europe. Very few mobile students from this region go to Latin America and the Caribbean, South and West Asia, or the Arab States.

The Arab States hosted nearly 2.9 percent of internationally mobile students in 2007; the region's share of the world total fell 0.4 percent over the period. Western Europe was the destination of 57 percent of the region's mobile students; 16 percent moved within the region and 15 percent went to North America. From 1999–2007, students from the Arab States increasingly moved within the region, to East Asia and the Pacific, and to South and West Asia; they were less likely to go to Western Europe, Central and Eastern Europe, North America, or Central Asia. Very few mobile students from this region go to Latin America and the Caribbean.

Sub-Saharan Africa hosted 2.6 percent of the world's mobile students in 2007, mostly in South Africa. No other region sends a measurable percentage of its mobile students to Sub-Saharan Africa. However, 23 percent of the region's own mobile students study there, and this percentage figure has risen since 1999. Of the rest, 50 percent go to Western Europe, 17 percent to North America, and 4 percent to East Asia and the Pacific, the only other region to have increased its share of SSA students.

Central Asia hosted nearly 2 percent of the world total. The region sent its biggest numbers of mobile students to Central and Eastern Europe (44 percent, down from 60 percent in 1999). The next-biggest numbers moved within the region (35 percent, up 6 percent), to Western Europe (12 percent, also up 6 percent), to North America (5 percent, up 1 percent), and to East Asia and the Pacific (3 percent, up 2 percent).

Latin America and the Caribbean also hosted nearly 2 percent of the world total in 2007. Mobile students from the region were most likely to go to North America (43 percent), followed by Western Europe (31 percent). Both of these regions, particularly North America, lost ground from 1999–2007, but the number of students moving within the region rose from 11 percent to 23 percent. Mobility to East Asia and the Pacific also rose. Very few students from Latin America and the Caribbean go to any other regions.

South and West Asia comes last in world share with 0.4 percent. The region's own mobile students prefer to go to North America (26 percent), Western Europe (31 percent), or East Asia and the Pacific (21 percent), though only the last-named has increased its share since 1999. From 1999–2007, the percentage of students moving within the region has halved, to 1.4 percent.

According to UNESCO figures, in 2007, 29 percent of the world's internationally mobile students originated in East Asia and the Pacific; 18 percent came from Western Europe and North America taken together; 11 percent from Central and Eastern Europe; 9 percent from South and West Asia; 8 percent from Sub-Saharan Africa; 7 percent from Arab States; 6 percent from Latin America and the Caribbean; 3.5 percent from Central Asia; and 9 percent were "origin unspecified." We noted earlier that some 2 percent of the world's tertiary students are internationally mobile, but some regions export significantly higher proportions of students. Sub-Saharan Africa leads this list, with about 5.8 percent of tertiary students studying abroad in 2007, followed by Central Asia with 5 percent.

TABLE 2.3: FOREIGN AND INTERNATIONAL STUDENTS ENROLLED IN TERTIARY EDUCATION, BY DESTINATION COUNTRY AND LEVEL OF STUDY (2008); GROWTH IN NUMBERS ENROLLED, BY DESTINATION COUNTRY (2000–2008)

		International Students				Foreign Students				Change Index 2000 (=100) to 2008
	Foreign Students 2008	% of All Tertiary	% of Type B	% of Type A	% of Adv Resch	% of All Tertiary	% of Type B	% of Type A	% of Adv Resch	
United States	624,474	3.4	1.0	3.4	28.1	n/a	n/a	n/a	n/a	131
United Kingdom	335,870	14.7	5.9	16.0	42.0	19.9	12.3	20.8	47.7	151
Germany	245,522	n/a	n/a	9.3	n/a	10.9	3.6	12.2	n/a	131
France	243,436	n/a	n/a	n/a	n/a	11.2	4.1	12.4	39.8	178
Australia	230,635	20.6	18.6	20.9	23.3	23.6	18.9	24.1	33.8	218
Canada	185,399	6.5	4.5	6.9	20.2	13.1	9.6	13.7	38.6	196
Russia	143,303	n/a	n/a	n/a	n/a	1.4	0.4	1.7	n/a	348
Japan	126,568	2.9	2.9	2.6	16.2	3.2	2.9	3.0	16.9	190
Italy	68,273	n/a	n/a	n/a	n/a	3.0	n/a	2.9	7.0	274
Spain	64,906	2.1	5.3	1.1	12.7	3.6	5.3	2.4	24.0	255
New Zealand	59,636	12.9	12.5	12.4	31.3	24.4	22.3	24.4	46.9	726
Austria	53,396	15.5	4.9	15.8	23.5	18.7	11.4	18.8	26.0	176
Switzerland	45,583	14.1	n/a	14.6	46.0	20.3	18.5	17.9	45.9	175
Belgium	42,484	8.6	6.3	9.7	21.4	12.2	9.0	13.7	31.2	109
Netherlands	40,795	5.0	n/a	5.1	n/a	6.8	n/a	6.9	n/a	291
Korea	40,322	n/a	n/a	n/a	n/a	1.3	0.6	1.4	6.6	1,195
Sweden	34,556	5.6	0.5	5.1	19.7	8.5	4.1	7.9	23.7	135
Czech Republic	27,907	n/a	n/a	n/a	n/a	7.1	1.1	7.5	9.9	510
Greece	26,158	n/a	n/a	n/a	n/a	4.1	4.5	4.1	n/a	304
Turkey	20,219	n/a	n/a	n/a	n/a	0.8	0.1	1.0	2.7	115

Source: UNESCO Institute for Statistics (2010). Global education digest 2010: Comparing education statistics across the world. Montreal: UNESCO-UIS. Tables C2.1 and C2.7 (www.uis.unesco.org).

Note: As in chart 2.1, the figures in the first and the final columns for United States, United Kingdom and Australia are for international rather than foreign students and the figure for Canada is for 2007 rather than 2008.

At what level of tertiary education do international students study?

Table 2.3 shows study levels for overseas students in popular destination countries, including all of those named in chart 2.1 except China and South Africa, excluded for a lack of directly comparable figures. For each country, this table shows the 2008 number of foreign students and the percentage of overseas students (international students, foreign students, or both, depending on what each country can provide) within the student body. Then it shows the percentages of international/foreign students within the student body for *Type A* tertiary courses—theory-based courses requiring three or more years of tertiary study, such as first (bachelor's) degrees and U.S. and UK second (master's) degrees; *Type B* tertiary courses—vocational courses, generally shorter than Type A but requiring at least two years of tertiary study, focusing on practical, technical, or occupational skills for direct entry into the labor market; and *Advanced Research* programs, such as Ph.D.s. The "Index of Change" in the final column shows which countries have most increased their numbers of overseas students from 2000–08.

Table 2.3 shows interesting differences between countries in the types and levels of tertiary programs on which international students are most likely to be found. Type B programs (shorter, more vocational) tend not to be as internationalized as Type A programs, except in Spain (where there is a higher proportion of overseas students in Type B programs), Japan, Switzerland, Greece, New Zealand, and Australia. Advanced research programs attract a greater percentage of overseas students than other academic programs (Type A) in many countries. International students constitute more than 40 percent of advanced research students in the UK and Switzerland; more than 30 percent in New Zealand; and more than 20 percent in the U.S., Canada, Austria, and Belgium. The proportion of foreign students doing advanced research is particularly high in France. Other countries that are relatively likely to attract international/foreign students for advanced research—as shown by an advanced research percentage at least three times as high as their Type A percentage—include Japan, Spain, Sweden, and South Korea.

The final column of table 2.3 indicates growth over the last eight years. As mentioned earlier, the average growth from 2000–08 for all countries reporting to OECD and UNESCO was 85 percent. The countries showing the least percentage growth were Belgium (9 percent), Turkey (15 percent), the U.S. and Germany (each with 31 percent), and Sweden (35 percent). Popular destinations that saw medium growth of 50–100 percent included (in ascending order) the UK, Switzerland, Austria, France, Japan, and Canada. All others at least doubled their numbers over the period; the most dramatic increases were nearly 250 percent in Russia, over 400 percent in the Czech Republic, over 600 percent in New Zealand, and over 1,000 percent in South Korea.

In what fields of study do international students enroll?

Chart 2.4, from UNESCO's *Global Education Digest 2009*, shows that in 2007 almost one in four mobile students (23 percent) was on a business and administration program. In order of popularity, 15 percent were enrolled in science; 14.4 percent in engineering, manufacturing and construction; and 13.9 percent in humanities and arts. All these subjects attract a higher proportion of international than of local students, whereas the next four in popularity order—social sciences and law, health and welfare, education, and services—are more popular with local students, perhaps because career requirements in these fields tend to be more country-specific. Agriculture is the major field least likely to attract international, and indeed local, students.

CHART 2.4: IN WHICH FIELD OF EDUCATION DO MOBILE STUDENTS ENROLL?

Distribution of tertiary enrolment by field of education and origin of students, 2007

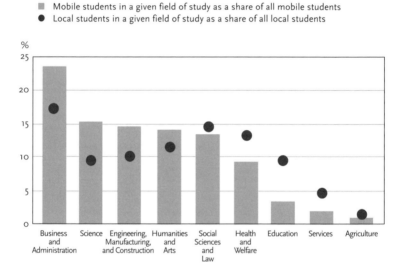

Notes: *Mobile students by field of education reported by participating countries represent 76% of total mobile students in 2007.*

Local students in host countries refer to students who are residents or citizens of the country in which they study.

Source: *UNESCO-UIS/OECD/Eurostat (UOE) and World Education Indicators (WEI) database. (stats.uis.unesco.org)*

As OECD figures for 2008 in *Education at a Glance 2010* demonstrate, however, different countries specialize in different fields when it comes to attracting international students. For example, social sciences, business, and law—which together attracted 36 percent of international students, according to UNESCO—attracted considerably more than this in Australia, Canada, Japan, the Netherlands, New Zealand, Portugal, Estonia, and France. Science programs attracted more international/foreign students than UNESCO's global average of 15 percent in Canada, Germany, Iceland, New Zealand, Sweden, Switzerland, the United States, and France. Germany, Portugal, Sweden, Switzerland, Slovenia, and the United States have more international students than the UNESCO average in engineering, manufacturing, and construction. Humanities and the arts attracted a much higher than average percentage of international students in Austria, Germany, Iceland, Japan, Norway, and France, as did health and welfare in Belgium, Denmark, Hungary, Spain, Poland, and Slovakia. Agriculture is particularly popular in Belgium, Hungary, and Estonia; education is especially popular in Slovakia.

Shorter-term tertiary mobility

So far we have relied on OECD and UNESCO statistics for our analysis of tertiary mobility. These statistics exclude students enrolled in a tertiary institution for less than a year. They effectively capture "diploma mobility," where students study the entire degree program at an institution in a country other than the country where they obtained their school-leaving certificates, but often fail to capture temporary mobility, or "credit mobility," where students go to another country for part of their studies, but return to their university of origin to graduate. This is a pity: a temporary move can be an equally valuable way for students to experience another system and culture. Arguably, individuals are more marketable and better prepared to compete in today's global labor market with a qualification incorporating elements from two systems. Some countries or groups of countries recognize the potential benefits of temporary mobility at tertiary level, encourage it (for example, through sponsored exchange schemes), and record it in their mobility statistics. Two prominent examples are the United States and the European Union.

In the United States, universities and colleges have a comprehensive system of credit accumulation and transfer that aids recognition of short-term study overseas as part of a degree. The Institute of International Education (IIE) collects figures on outward "credit" mobility through annual surveys of higher education institutions. In *Open Doors 2010*, IIE reports that 260,327 U.S. students studied abroad for academic credit in 2008/9. This was a drop of 0.8 percent over 2007/8, the first drop in 25 years. Of the 2008/9 students abroad, 11.8 percent of these were graduate students (including doctoral and professional students), and 1.1 percent were associate's students. Among the 87.1 percent who were undergraduates, the highest numbers (36.8 percent) were in their junior year (the third year of the typical U.S. four-year bachelor's degree). IIE estimates that around 10 percent of all U.S. undergraduate students studied abroad in 2008/9.

IIE's 2008/9 survey found that only 4.3 percent of the 260,327 U.S. students studying abroad did so for a full academic or calendar year—meaning that 96 percent of the U.S.'s outward "credit" mobility will not be picked up in OECD/UNESCO statistics. 41.1 percent of outgoing students went abroad for one or two quarters or a semester (mid-length), and 54.7 percent went for the summer, January term, or eight weeks or less (short-term). Over the past 15 years, the numbers doing a short-term study period abroad have quadrupled, the numbers doing a mid-length study period abroad have more than doubled, and the numbers going abroad for a full year have remained steady or slightly declined.

Table 2.4 shows the top 25 destination countries for U.S. students abroad in 2008/9, their percentages of the total, and how the numbers each country received had changed since 2007/8. The UK continues to be the most popular, with 12 percent, followed by Italy, Spain, and France, but all their numbers fell in the latest year—as did numbers received by all other Western European countries in the top 25 except the Netherlands (22nd) and Denmark (23rd). Others whose numbers fell included Mexico, with a 26 percent drop, and India, with a 14 percent drop. Countries becoming significantly more popular included China (5th); Costa Rica (10th); and several less traditional destinations with increases of more than 10 percent, including Argentina, South Africa, Chile, Peru, and South Korea.

The most popular fields for U.S. study abroad in 2008/9 were social sciences (21 percent), business and management (20 percent), and humanities (12 percent). These

TABLE 2.4: DESTINATIONS OF U.S. STUDY ABROAD STUDENTS (2008/9, CHANGES FROM 2007/8)

RANK	DESTINATION COUNTRY	2008/9 NUMBERS	2008/9 % OF TOTAL	CHANGE ON 2007/8 %	RANK	DESTINATION COUNTRY	2008/9 NUMBERS	2008/9 % OF TOTAL	CHANGE ON 2007/8 %
1.	United Kingdom	31,342	12.0	- 6.0	14.	Czech Republic	3,664	1.4	+ 7.2
2.	Italy	27,362	10.5	- 10.8	15.	Greece	3,616	1.4	- 6.0
3.	Spain	24,169	9.3	- 4.1	16.	Chile	3,503	1.3	+ 27.9
4.	France	16,910	6.5	- 2.5	17.	Ecuador	2,859	1.1	+ 1.6
5.	China	13,674	5.3	+ 3.9	18.	Austria	2,836	1.1	- 15.5
6.	Australia	11,140	4.3	+ 0.9	19.	Brazil	2,777	1.1	+ 2.0
7.	Germany	8,330	3.2	+ 0.9	20.	New Zealand	2,769	1.1	+ 5.3
8.	Mexico	7,320	2.8	- 26.3	21.	India	2,690	1.0	- 14.5
9.	Ireland	6,858	2.6	- 0.3	22.	Netherlands	2,318	0.9	+ 13.7
10.	Costa Rica	6,363	2.4	+ 4.4	23.	Denmark	2,244	0.9	+ 21.0
11.	Japan	5,784	2.2	+ 1.3	24.	Peru	2,163	0.8	+ 32.1
12.	Argentina	4,705	1.8	+14.5	25.	South Korea	2,062	0.8	+ 29.1
13.	South Africa	4,160	1.6	+12.4		World	260,327	100	- 0.8

Source: Chow, P. and Bhandari, R. (2010). Open doors 2010: Report on international educational exchange. New York: Institute of International Education.

were followed by fine or applied arts (7 percent), physical and life sciences (7 percent), foreign languages (6 percent), health (5 percent), education (4 percent), engineering (3 percent), math and computer science (2 percent), and agriculture (1 percent).

The U.S. encourages inward temporary mobility for a range of purposes, most of them related to education, through its longstanding Exchange Visitor visa arrangements. Our U.S. country study in part II includes an analysis of all Exchange Visitors coming to the U.S. for educational purposes.

The European Union's Erasmus program enables higher education students from countries in the EU, the European Economic Area, and Turkey to study and work abroad. As the Erasmus website notes:

> Many studies show that a period spent abroad not only enriches students' lives in the academic and professional fields, but can also improve language learning, intercultural skills, self-reliance and self-awareness. Their experiences give students a better sense of what it means to be a European citizen. In addition, many employers highly value such a period abroad, which increases the students' employability and job prospects ("Erasmus Programme," n.d.).

The vast majority of European universities take part in Erasmus. More than 4,000 higher education institutions in 33 countries currently participate, and more are waiting to join. Students enrolled at these institutions can study abroad at other participating institutions for 3–12 months with an Erasmus grant. Since 2007, registered students may also undertake work placements in enterprises overseas.

Table 2.5 shows the numbers of students taking short-term study or work placements elsewhere in Europe in 2008/9, supported by Erasmus. The table shows flows into and out of the most important host countries and within the wider European area.

The top five host countries, in this order, were Spain, France, Germany, the United Kingdom, and Italy. The top five sending countries, in this order, were France, Germany, Spain, Italy, and the United Kingdom. Because Erasmus is in principle an exchange scheme, it aims for a roughly even balance between numbers exported and imported by each country. This is not easy to achieve for popular destinations whose students may be reluctant to travel, like the UK, which in 2008/9 hosted 10.5 percent of Erasmus movers but originated 5.5 percent. Another generous host is Sweden, which hosted 4.5 percent and sent 1.4 percent. Major countries that sent more students than they received included France, Germany, and Italy.

The Erasmus scheme has had a major impact on student mobility. More than 2.2 million individuals have studied abroad under its auspices since it started in 1987. According to the Erasmus website, the scheme has helped to drive the modernization of higher education institutions and systems in Europe and inspired the establishment of the Bologna process.

Host \ Origin	Sp (%)	Fr (%)	Ge (%)	UK (%)	It (%)	Sw (%)	N (%)	B (%)	Fi (%)	O (%)	TOTAL (%)
Spain (Sp)		3,714	2,990	3,119	6,532	979	1,211	1,409	792	6,659	27,405 (13.8)
France (Fr)	6,262		3,412	5,681 ,	1,789	1,632	1,139	739	987	6,642	28,283 (14.2)
Germany (Ge)	5,666	4,818		3,849	1,750	2,275	935	502	1,179	6,920	27,894 (14.0)
United Kingdom	2,385	3,537	1,657		809	315	440	189	224	1,270	10,826 (5.5)
Italy (It)	7,044	3,004	1,836	1604		514	671	712	436	3,555	19,376 (9.8)
Sweden (Sw)	309	469	398	491	148		215	77	16	561	2,684 (1.4)
Netherlands (N)	1,266	664	674	1,041	379	574		573	291	1,543	7,005 (3.5)
Belgium (B)	1,525	977	392	450	482	214	365		248	1,292	5,945 (3.0)
Finland (Fi)	692	429	645	561	180	178	308	174		1,244	4,411 (2.2)
Other (O)	8,029	7,003	9,935	4,055	5,427	2,159	27,98	2,471	2,433		64,739
TOTAL	33,178 (16.7)	24,615 (12.4)	21,939 (11.0)	20,851 (10.5)	17,496 (8.8)	8,840 (4.5)	8,082 (4.1)	6,846 (3.3)	6,606 (3.4)	50,115 (25.2)	198,568 (100)

Source: Erasmus website, http://ec.europa.eu/education/lifelong-learning-programme

Another relevant EU mobility scheme is Erasmus Mundus, a mobility program that aims to promote dialogue and understanding through cooperation between higher education institutions in Europe and institutions in other regions. This program provides support to higher education institutions that wish to implement joint programs at the graduate level or to set up inter-institutional cooperation partnerships between universities from Europe and from targeted non-European countries. It also supports individual students, researchers, and university staff who wish to spend a study/research/teaching period in the context of one of the joint programs or cooperation partnerships, and helps organizations active in the field of higher education that wish to develop projects aimed at enhancing the attractiveness, profile, visibility, and image of European higher education worldwide.

In 2008/9 Erasmus Mundus sponsored 2,031 students from 116 non-European countries to come to Europe. The top 15 sending countries were China (244), India (164), Brazil (112), Ethiopia (104), Mexico (84), Russia (81), the United States (75), Bangladesh (69), Indonesia (61), Colombia (58), Pakistan (54), Canada (53), Iran (50), Serbia (46), and the Philippines (41).

Chapter 3

GLOBAL STUDENT MOBILITY IN NON-TERTIARY EDUCATION

Introduction

This chapter assesses what is known about global student mobility at levels other than tertiary. It considers mobility at upper secondary school level; mobility in post-secondary non-tertiary education; mobility among teachers, researchers, scholars, professors, and other academic staff; and mobility for other broadly education-related purposes. Sadly, mobility at these levels is poorly documented. Very few countries collect information on this mobility, and what is collected is not internationally comparable.

Mobility at secondary school level

OECD's statistical database contains some information on upper secondary students from overseas enrolled to study in OECD countries for a year or more. However, as noted in chapter 2, different countries record their figures for overseas students in different ways, if they record them at all. For 2008, the latest available year, 22 OECD countries recorded figures for *foreign* upper secondary students (i.e., all those who are not citizens of the country, regardless of whether they already live there). Only 7 of the smaller OECD countries recorded figures for *international* secondary students (i.e., all those who are not residents of the country). All 7 of these countries were among the 22 with figures available for foreign secondary students.

As mentioned in Chapter 2, OECD and UNESCO ask all their reporting countries to report numbers of international rather than foreign students if possible, because the foreign student basis overstates mobile student numbers by including long-term residents. This is even more likely to be so at secondary than at tertiary level. At secondary level, we would expect most of the non-citizen students in secondary schools to be there because their families had taken up residence in the country concerned, whether permanently or temporarily. Other reasons, such as a decision to broaden personal experience through study abroad or to facilitate entry into an overseas university system, are likely to be relevant only for a minority of students. These two reasons no doubt apply to some students, particularly if they are going to or coming from the United States, which has a tradition of encouraging "high school years abroad" for residents and visitors. But we would expect those students to be a small minority of all upper secondary school students studying outside their country of citizenship.

This expectation is borne out if we compare numbers for foreign and international upper secondary students in the seven OECD countries that record data for both categories. The information is in table 3.1. In all the countries shown, fewer than half of the foreign students are international (i.e., internationally mobile) students, and in four of the countries the ratio is as low as 1:10 or 1:20. The variability of the relationship between foreign and international student numbers suggests that we cannot place any reliance on "foreign student" information as a true guide to mobility at the upper secondary school level. Nor do these seven countries offer much of a guide to what is happening globally, given that they are relatively small countries, all but one in Western/Central Europe; that none of them is in the top 10 destinations for tertiary mobility; and that a check of figures from previous years (not shown) reveals surprising year-on-year changes, raising questions about the reliability of the data.

TABLE 3.1: FOREIGN AND INTERNATIONAL UPPER SECONDARY STUDENTS IN SELECTED OECD COUNTRIES (2008)

COUNTRY	FOREIGN STUDENTS 2008	INTERNATIONAL STUDENTS 2008 (AS % OF FOREIGN STUDENTS)
Austria	26,613	2,803 (10.5)
Belgium	35,938	9,121 (25.3)
Denmark	13,211	612 (4.6)
Luxembourg	7,522	393 (5.2)
New Zealand	20,339	9,464 (46.5)
Norway	9,994	960 (9.6)
Slovakia	330	163 (49.4)

Source: OECD (2010). Education at a glance: OECD indicators 2010. Paris: OECD.

EU and EEA countries participate in a scheme called Comenius, the equivalent for schools of the Erasmus scheme for higher education. Individual pupil mobility is an important element: schools in different European countries form partnerships and their pupils go on exchange visits to each other's countries. According to a 2008 report, *Mobility Creates Opportunities*, "in 2006 alone, 12,430 schools took part in approximately 3,000 school partnerships. Within these projects more than 90,000 pupils and teachers had the chance to visit their partner schools. Out of them 21,100 pupils went on a class exchange and spent two weeks in their partner school, experiencing everyday school life abroad."

Table 3.2 shows the numbers of school pupils from each country who went to another scheme country under the Comenius school partnerships set up in 2007. Of the sizeable total of 116,808 pupils traveling, nearly half (81,275) were from Germany. Spain, Italy, and Poland were also enthusiastic participants in the scheme. The UK and Ireland seem less so, perhaps because their pupils tend to be less fluent in foreign languages than those in most European countries.

Most of the pupils in table 3.2 travelled abroad for very short periods of 2–3 weeks. Comenius has now set up an additional Individual Pupil Mobility scheme under which secondary school students from participating countries will travel abroad for longer periods—a term, a semester, perhaps a year—but figures for numbers participating are not yet available.

The United States has a tradition of encouraging "high school years abroad" and boasts a number of organizations in the business of arranging and supporting

TABLE 3.2: COUNTRIES OF ORIGIN AND NUMBERS OF SCHOOL PUPILS TRAVELING TO ANOTHER EU/EEA COUNTRY UNDER COMENIUS SCHEME (APPLICATIONS SUBMITTED UNDER 2007 CALL FOR PROPOSALS)

COUNTRY	NUMBERS	COUNTRY	NUMBERS
1. Germany	81,275	15. Austria	993
2. Spain	5,012	16. Norway	851
3. Italy	4,753	17. Lithuania	829
4. Poland	3,707	18. Bulgaria	800
5. France	1,810	19. Greece	727
6. Finland	1,781	20. Latvia	646
7. Czech Republic	1,774	21. United Kingdom	644
8. Sweden	1,765	22. Slovenia	415
9. Turkey	1,676	23. Estonia	403
10. Romania	1,403	24. Cyprus	334
11. Hungary	1,382	25. Ireland	258
12. Slovakia	1,187	26. Luxembourg	183
13. Portugal	1,119	27. Iceland	57
14. Belgium	1,024	Total	116,808

Source: EU Comenius Unit

international mobility for that purpose. The U.S. country study in part II notes that 29,857 secondary students completed stays in the U.S. under Exchange Visitor arrangements during 2006; 29,446 in 2007; 28,695 in 2008; and 27,589 in 2009. The top 10 sending countries in 2009 were Germany, Brazil, China, Thailand, South Korea, Norway, Italy, Spain, Japan, and Denmark. Secondary students also enter the U.S. as Student Visitors: 24,988 overseas pupils on Student Visitor visas were enrolled at secondary/high schools in the U.S. at the end of June 2010.

The government of Australia is probably unique in publishing a wide array of useful statistics on incoming international students, covering mobility at all educational levels. From these statistics (Australian Education International (AEI) Student Enrollment Data, extracted September 2010) we know that 25,095 international students enrolled in Australian schools in 2005; 24,471 in 2006; 26,782 in 2007; 28,313 in 2008; and 27,506 in 2009. We also know that in 2010, up to and including the month of August, there were 23,414 international students enrolled in Australian schools, the top 10 sending places of origin being China, South Korea, Vietnam, Germany, Japan, Malaysia, Hong Kong, Thailand, Taiwan, and Indonesia. Out of these 2010 enrollments, 9,989 were commencements. For commencements, the top 6 sending places of origin were the same as for enrollments, but then Brazil was 7th, Thailand 8th, Papua New Guinea 9th, and Taiwan 10th.

Postsecondary non-tertiary education, including vocational education

Here again, OECD has some figures for postsecondary non-tertiary students from overseas studying in OECD countries for one year or more, but they are far from complete or comprehensive and are not always easy to reconcile with information on these countries from other sources. Only 10 countries have supplied figures on international (as opposed to foreign) students—the seven countries in table 3.1 plus Australia, Iceland, and Sweden. The figures for these countries are shown in table 3.3.

The number of OECD countries able to supply figures for international postsecondary non-tertiary students—though higher than the number able to contribute figures on international school students—is still only half of the number able to supply figures on international tertiary students. This is partly because many countries (the U.S. is just one example) regard all study undertaken after graduating from upper secondary or high school as tertiary study. Country comparisons are also complicated by the fact that countries have different ways of providing vocational education and training (VET) below tertiary level. Some offer courses leading to vocational and technical qualifications to young people still in upper secondary schools, often in separate vocational/technical schools or streams. In these countries, any international students would appear in the school statistics. In others, the international students would appear in the postsecondary non-tertiary statistics, because vocational or technical qualifications are usually gained after leaving school and enrolling in a further education or technical college.

TABLE 3.3: INTERNATIONAL POSTSECONDARY
NON-TERTIARY STUDENTS IN OECD COUNTRIES
(2008)

COUNTRY	INTERNATIONAL STUDENTS 2008
New Zealand	4,484
Australia	4,120
Belgium	2,428
Sweden	603
Austria	429
Luxembourg	184
Norway	43
Denmark	37
Iceland	17
Slovakia	9

Source: OECD (2010). Education at a glance: OECD
indicators 2010. *Paris: OECD.*

The United Kingdom is an example of the second type of country. From the age of 16, young people may choose to leave school and pursue any type of upper secondary qualification—vocational/technical or general—in further education (FE) colleges. Some FE colleges, known as sixth form colleges, offer young people very similar courses and academic qualifications to those available to 16- to 18-year-olds in schools—but in a wider range of subjects and a more adult environment. Table 3.4 shows the total number of international students enrolled in UK further education colleges in 2006/7, as well as the top sending countries.

It is likely that the majority of the international students in table 3.4 would have been studying for qualifications below tertiary level—some of them, no doubt, taking English language courses. The website of Universities UK, the organization that represents higher education institutions, states that altogether over 600,000 learners a year come to the UK to learn English—though the student visa changes reported in chapter 5 are likely to reduce the numbers in future.

Australia's government statistics on international student enrollment, as well as showing numbers enrolled in higher education and schools, include three other student categories that we will consider in this section, though some may include tertiary-level courses. The categories are VET, ELICOS (English Language Intensive

TABLE 3.4: INTERNATIONAL STUDENTS IN UK
FURTHER EDUCATION COLLEGES (2006/7)

	2006/7
Total International Students	84,340
Of which:	
EU	46,385
Non-EU	37,955
Top Sending Countries:	
1. Poland	16,455
2. India	4,735
3. Ireland	4,580
4. China	3,985
5. Spain	3,970
6. Italy	3,355
7. France	3,050
8. Slovakia	2,615
9. Germany	2,380
10. Czech Republic	2,100
11. Pakistan	1,920
12. Lithuania	1,480
13. Hungary	1,375
14. Portugal	1,260
15. Japan	1,230
16. Nigeria	1,085

Source: Source: UK Council for International Student
Affairs (UKCISA)

Courses for Overseas Students), and Other (defined as including enabling, foundation, and non-award courses). Numbers enrolled in these three categories in 2005–09 are shown in table 3.5. They attracted 63 percent of the 631,935 international students enrolled in Australia in 2009; the remaining 230,830 were in higher education.

TABLE 3.5: INTERNATIONAL STUDENTS IN AUSTRALIA, EXCLUDING HE AND
SCHOOL STUDENTS (2005–09)

SECTOR	2005	2006	2007	2008	2009
VET	65,580	82,546	119,707	174,395	232,475
ELICOS	64,255	76,469	101,487	125,764	135,141
Other	26,564	26,843	27,809	31,248	33,489
Total	156,399	185,858	249,003	331,407	401,105

Source: Australian Education International (AEI) Student Enrolment Data, extracted
September 2010

As the table shows, the numbers of international students have grown steadily from year to year in all three categories, but particularly in VET, where Australia seems to have found a market niche. The impressive growth of 25 percent in Australia's numbers of international higher education students over the same period—from 162,689 in 2005 to 203,324 in 2009—is outstripped by the growth in ELICOS (110 percent) and VET (254 percent). There are now more VET than higher education students coming to Australia, though here too, recent visa policy changes may alter the position in future (see chapter 5).

According to the AEI website, in 2009 Asian countries dominated VET activity with 85.0 percent of enrollments and 84.7 percent of commencements. India was the top source country, with a 34.3 percent share of enrollments and a 34.6 percent share of commencements, followed by China, with shares of 14.5 percent and 14.6 percent. No other source country in this sector individually contributed more than 10 percent of enrollments or commencements. Management and commerce was the largest broad field of education in VET, with 46.0 percent of enrollments and 39.9 percent of commencements. Food, hospitality and personal services ranked second, contributing 24.4 percent and 28.7 percent. All other broad fields of education contributed less than 10 percent of enrollments and commencements.

At the time of writing, full statistics for 2010 are not available, but AEI has published figures for the 11 months to November 2010, compared to the same 11 months in 2009. For reasons already mentioned in chapter 1, resulting from national policy changes discussed in chapter 5, total VET enrollments grew by just 0.2 percent (though remaining higher in absolute numbers than higher education enrollments, which rose 8.5 percent). VET commencements fell by 8.2 percent. ELICOS saw dramatic declines in both enrollments (17.6 percent) and commencements (21.3 percent); enrollments and commencements in the Other category also fell, though less dramatically.

Mobility of professors and other academic staff, researchers, and scholars

The globalization of higher education means that large numbers of academic staff, researchers, and scholars take postings overseas. For example, according to a recent study (Kim & Locke, 2010), 27 percent of full-time academic staff appointed in the UK in 2007/08 came from outside the UK. The most common countries of origin for these overseas academics in UK posts were Germany, Ireland, the United States, China, Italy, France, and Greece. While it could be argued that all international movers in professions connected with education are being internationally mobile for educational purposes, this study is more concerned with those who move as part of their learning than with those who move to take up jobs. Therefore, we will focus on the information available on movements of academics, researchers, and scholars under exchange-type schemes.

TABLE 3.6: INWARD AND OUTWARD MOBILITY OF ACADEMIC STAFF UNDER EU ERASMUS SCHEME (2008/9)

Host / Origin	PL (%)	SP (%)	GE (%)	FR (%)	CZ (%)	IT (%)	UK (%)	FI (%)	RO (%)	B (%)	TOTAL (%)
Poland (Pl)		466	634	276	349	393	242	121	41	82	4,340 (11.8)
Spain (Sp)	135		374	480	68	937	302	131	54	123	3,695 (10.2)
Germany (Ge)	276	339		281	124	221	248	205	124	45	3,134 (8.6)
France (Fr)	229	434	243		116	346	191	65	340	109	2,840 (7.8)
Czech Rep (Cz)	234	168	324	175		101	158	131	26	46	2,580 (7.1)
Italy (It)	99	487	146	289	29		126	40	63	56	1,920 (5.3)
United Kingdom	78	183	234	181	76	128		144	34	33	1,771 (4.9)
Finland (Fi)	54	166	216	105	59	81	174		23	102	1,718 (4.7)
Romania (Ro)	18	120	39	358	28	154	20	28	1	45	1,261 (3.5)
Belgium (B)	70	130	48	175	21	66	39	116	45		1,224 (3.4)
TOTAL, ALL COUNTRIES	1,904 (5.2)	3,446 (9.5)	3,777 (10.4)	3,076 (8.4)	1,526 (4.2)	3,224 (8.9)	2,327 (6.4)	1,720 (4.7)	1,060 (2.9)	1,053 (2.9)	36,388 (100)

Source: Erasmus website, http://ec.europa.eu/education/lifelong-learning-programme

The <u>European Union</u> promotes mobility of academic staff within the EU, EEA, and Turkey as part of the Erasmus program (already discussed in chapter 2 in connection with mobility of tertiary students). Table 3.6 shows the total numbers involved in 2008/9 and the movements in and out of the top 10 sending countries, which were led by Poland, Spain, Germany, France, and the Czech Republic.

As also mentioned in chapter 2, one of the purposes of the EU's Erasmus Mundus program is to support researchers and university staff from non-European countries who wish to study, research, or teach in a European higher education institution. In 2008/9, Erasmus Mundus supported 456 scholars from 61 non-European countries. The top 10 sending countries were the United States (77), India (39), Brazil (32), China (30), Canada (26), Australia (25), Japan (18), Russia (18), Argentina (12), and Mexico (12).

Information is also available on academics and scholars from other countries who enter the <u>United States</u> for limited periods. The first source is information on those who hold Exchange Visitor (J-1) visas. Table 3.7 is taken from the U.S. country study in part II. It sets out the numbers of professors (a term used to cover all academic staff), researchers, and short-term scholars completing their Exchange Visitor programs in 2009. When comparing numbers in different groups it should be noted that professors and researchers can remain in the U.S. for five years as Exchange Visitors, but short-term scholars can remain no longer than six months. The shorter the maximum duration of visits, the more individuals are likely to feature among the completions in any given year.

As the table shows, China sent by far the biggest numbers in all three groups. South Korea, ranking 2nd for professors and researchers, and Germany, ranking 2nd for short-term scholars, appear in all three top 10 lists, as do Italy, France, and Spain. Countries appearing in two of the three lists include Japan (3rd for researchers and 7th for professors), India (4th for researchers and 6th for short-term scholars), the United Kingdom, and Brazil.

Our second source is the survey-based information published by IIE in *Open Doors* on international scholars being hosted by U.S. higher education institutions. *Open Doors 2010* reported that in 2009/10 there were 115,098 international scholars in U.S. HE institutions, a 1.5 percent increase on the previous year; that the leading countries of origin were China (25.6 percent), India (10.0 percent) and South Korea (8.5 percent), followed by Germany, Japan, Canada, France, Italy, the UK, Spain, and Brazil each sending between 2 and 5 percent; that the greatest numbers were in the field of Biological and Biomedical Sciences (23 percent), followed by Health Sciences (18 percent); and that Harvard hosted the highest numbers (4,203).

Of these 115,098 international scholars, 77 percent were doing research, 9 percent were engaged in teaching, and another 6 percent were engaged in both teaching and research. Of the total, 63 percent were on Exchange Visitor (J-1) visas—these individuals will also have been included in figures in table 3.7 if they completed their programs in 2009—and 30 percent were on H-1B visas, another type of nonimmigrant visa that allows a U.S. organization to employ foreign individuals for up to six years in occupations requiring a high degree of specialized knowledge. The remaining 7 percent had some other visa status. Sixty-four percent were male; 36 percent were female.

TABLE 3.7: PROFESSORS, RESEARCHERS AND SCHOLARS (EXCHANGE VISITORS) IN THE U.S. (2009 COMPLETION TOTALS AND TOP 10 PLACES OF ORIGIN)

	PROFESSORS (ACADEMICS)		RESEARCHERS		SHORT-TERM SCHOLARS	
TOTALS 2009 (COMPLETIONS)	1,369		26,370		18,106	
TOP 10 SENDING COUNTRIES:						
1.	China	362	China	7,912	China	2,792
2.	South Korea	111	South Korea	2,968	Germany	1,370
3.	Germany	89	Japan	1,574	Italy	944
4.	France	85	India	1,399	France	885
5.	Italy	61	Germany	1,289	Spain	797
6.	United Kingdom	50	Italy	1,018	India	600
7.	Japan	47	France	977	United Kingdom	566
8.	Spain	46	Brazil	702	South Korea	490
9.	Canada	36	Spain	634	Brazil	481
10.	Israel	36	Taiwan	573	Netherlands	406

Source: U.S. Department of State information on J-1 visas supplied to the authors

Mobility of teachers

The European Union/European Economic Area Comenius scheme, already mentioned in relation to school students, also provides European mobility opportunities for school teachers undertaking in-service training and for student teachers on Comenius Assistantships. Table 3.8 shows the numbers of teachers and student teachers from each country participating. The total numbers traveling for training were greatest in the latest year, 2009, when 1,173 student teachers and 10,606 qualified teachers participated. In that year, Turkey sent the most student teachers, followed by Italy and Germany. Spain sent the most teachers, followed by France, Germany, and the United Kingdom.

TABLE 3.8: TEACHERS AND STUDENT TEACHERS TRAINING IN ANOTHER EU/EEA COUNTRY UNDER THE COMENIUS SCHEME, BY COUNTRY OF ORIGIN (2007–09)

Country	ASSISTANTSHIPS FOR STUDENT TEACHERS			IN-SERVICE TEACHER TRAINING		
	2007	2008	2009	2007	2008	2009
Austria	7	18	10	291	299	261
Belgium	57	71	64	106	179	196
Bulgaria	18	22	11	136	163	115
Cyprus	4	4	3	48	49	49
Czech Republic	25	25	28	217	249	287
Denmark	22	18	11	176	182	178
Estonia	8	5	9	62	63	77
Finland	26	29	24	125	204	259
France	80	110	101	727	1,052	1,166
Germany	121	136	127	911	1,120	1,091
Greece	15	9	15	203	208	178
Hungary	38	33	40	222	193	190
Iceland	1	2	3	62	65	83
Ireland	22	21	18	42	47	72
Italy	108	114	135	835	709	731
Latvia	14	8	10	107	106	125
Liechtenstein	0	2	1	7	8	4
Lithuania	12	14	12	116	108	108
Luxembourg	4	5	2	9	15	14
Malta	0	0	0	29	31	0
Netherlands	20	11	10	408	372	375
Norway	15	10	12	109	98	137
Poland	116	121	95	481	671	702
Portugal	19	10	14	229	254	249
Romania	14	20	22	343	367	765
Slovakia	26	15	17	61	66	86
Slovenia	13	8	11	75	65	56
Spain	75	53	116	1,005	1,184	1,324
Sweden	20	20	17	237	480	449
Turkey	104	113	145	227	485	414
United Kingdom	99	78	90	1,128	1,156	865
Total	**1,103**	**1,105**	**1,173**	**8,734**	**10,248**	**10,606**

Source: EU Comenius Unit

United States Exchange Visitor arrangements include a scheme for incoming teachers in schools. Table 3.9 shows the top 10 sending countries in 2009. The list is led by France, Spain, and China. It also features several countries not in the tertiary education top 10 lists, such as Mexico, Colombia, Turkey, Argentina, and Uruguay.

TABLE 3.9: TEACHERS (EXCHANGE VISITORS) IN THE U.S.: TOP 10 COUNTRIES OF ORIGIN AND TOTAL (2009)

1. France	227	6. Colombia	59
2. Spain	215	7. Turkey	43
3. China	149	8. Argentina	37
4. Mexico	115	9. Israel	35
5. India	73	10. Uruguay	35
		TOTAL	1,472

Source: U.S. Department of State information on J-1 visas supplied to the authors

Other movers for educational purposes

The United States Exchange Visitor scheme encompasses a number of other groups regarded as moving to the U.S. for educational purposes, either because their program must include a study component or because they must be in secondary or tertiary education to qualify for the Exchange Visitor visa. These groups include Au Pairs, Camp Counselors, Summer Work/Travelers, Interns, and Trainees. All are fully discussed in the U.S. country study in part II.

Chapter 4

WHY STUDENTS MOVE AND
HOW THEY CHOOSE DESTINATIONS

This chapter considers the "push factors" that drive young people to move from their home countries for education-related purposes, as well as the "pull factors" that attract them to particular destination countries. Because so much of the data on global mobility for education purposes relates to tertiary education, we will inevitably have more to say about mobility at the tertiary stage.

Why students move: Push factors

Recent studies agree that the reasons for mobility are many and varied (see, for example, OECD, 2010, and UNESCO, 2009). A big push factor, naturally, is that students cannot find what they want at home. This may have to do with the quantity/quality, or range of educational opportunities available in the home country.

The global demand for post-compulsory education has grown massively in recent years, even if we judge demand solely from supply. UNESCO's *Global Education Digest 2009*, which focused on global trends in tertiary education, records rises in numbers enrolled for a year or more from 28.6 million in 1970, to 100.8 million in 2000, to 152.5 million in 2007. The number of tertiary students grew quickest in the most recent period, the seven years from 2000 to 2007, when it rose by 51.7 million people, or more than 50 percent. As we noted in chapter 2, the impressive growth in numbers of internationally mobile tertiary students from 1999–2007 simply tracked the impressive worldwide growth in tertiary enrollment, while the proportion of tertiary students who moved to another country remained constant at around 2 percent.

Clearly, there has been a big global increase in tertiary provision. What we do not know is how far the growth in individual countries has produced enough places to meet the demands of their populations, or whether the places provided give the people what they want in terms of quality, level, subject field, accessibility, and subsequent job opportunities. If local provision is deficient in any of these respects, students will think about moving. If other countries offer study opportunities on attractive terms and no major obstacles face the students themselves, they will move. Obstacles that can prevent push factors from having a mobility result—which we will call "anti-push factors"—are considered below.

How might we tell whether countries are giving their populations what they want by way of tertiary opportunities? The numbers of mobile students originating in each country are relevant, of course—table 2.1 listed all the countries recorded by OECD as having 20,000 or more of their citizens enrolled in other countries' tertiary systems in 2008. However, apart from the perennial problem that these figures represent students regarded as "foreign" by the destination country—which could include some long-term residents of that country, if it has sizeable numbers of residents who are not also citizens—absolute numbers need to be related to the size of each originating country's population, and particularly to its population of young people in the typical tertiary study age group. Trends in numbers over a period need also to be related to trends in numbers in the tertiary age groups over that same period. In many developed countries, including Japan, the young population has been declining, whereas in most developing countries it has been rising.

UNESCO's Institute for Statistics has found an interesting way of shedding light on whether countries are meeting the demands of their tertiary-age populations: comparing the average annual growth in the numbers of internationally mobile students from each country with the average annual growth in that country's numbers in tertiary education at home, over the period 1999–2007 (UNESCO, 2009, p. 38). Of the 79 countries in the analysis (which, sadly, excludes some important sending countries like India, Germany, Russia, and Canada for lack of data), 78 registered some measurable annual growth in domestic tertiary enrollment, the exception being Qatar. For international tertiary mobility, the countries fell into three groups.

In the smallest group, of 14 countries, local tertiary enrollment had grown on an annual basis while international tertiary enrollment had declined. In Japan, Austria, Italy, and Denmark, the decline in international enrollment was actually bigger than the growth in domestic enrollment. We might conclude that these countries and most of the others in the group of 14 are broadly giving their people what they want in terms of tertiary opportunities. This fits with other evidence in the cases of the countries just mentioned as well as in Ireland, Sweden, Norway, the United Kingdom, the Netherlands, and New Zealand; it is possible in the cases of Croatia and Turkey; but is very doubtful in the case of the Kyrgyz Republic (OECD, 2011).

In another group of 38 countries, both domestic and international enrollment grew but the number of outbound mobile students grew slower than local tertiary enrollment. This group of 38 includes several of the top 40 sending countries for tertiary students listed in table 2.1. They are China, whose international enrollments grew by over 15 percent per annum but whose local enrollments grew by a staggering 19 percent per annum, beaten only by Cuba and Laos; Romania (international 10 percent p.a., local 11 percent p.a.); Kazakhstan (international 7 percent p.a., local 12 percent p.a.); Brazil (international 3 percent p.a., local 10 percent p.a.); Thailand (international 3 percent p.a., local 4 percent p.a.); Iran (international 1 percent p.a., local 10 percent p.a.); Morocco (international 1 percent p.a., local 4 percent p.a.);

and France (both rates just over 1 percent p.a.). Countries in this group may be meeting many of their citizens' demands for tertiary education, particularly where rates of both local and international growth are low (France, Belgium); but there could well be unmet needs impelling significant numbers of citizens to look overseas.

In the third group of 25 countries, the number of outbound mobile students grew faster than local tertiary enrollment. In this group, top 40 sending countries included Slovakia, with an astonishing annual international mobility growth rate of 23 percent; Vietnam (international growth rate 17 percent p.a.); Belarus (international growth rate 12 percent p.a.); Poland, Ukraine, Colombia, Australia, Mexico, and South Korea (international growth rates all between 10 percent and 5 percent p.a.); and the United States (only just in this group because its international growth rate was only marginally ahead of its local growth rate, both being around 3 percent p.a.). Also in this group are Mongolia, whose high international growth rate of 15 percent p.a. is explained by starting from an extremely low base; several other former Soviet Union countries that needed time to rebuild their own education systems after the breakup of the USSR and have largely discovered the benefits of international educational mobility since independence; El Salvador, Yemen, Bangladesh, and Uruguay. Finally, the group includes Qatar, where international mobility plays an important part in meeting its tertiary growth needs, with an international growth rate of 6 percent annually.

In the case of these 25 countries, where the number of outbound mobile students grew faster than local tertiary enrollment, we might conclude that popular demand for tertiary education outstripped local supply over the period 1999–2007, or that some types of demand could not be satisfactorily met within the country, or both. It seems from other evidence that this is true of many countries among the 25. Some of them have national plans and policies intended to bridge gaps in their provision and bring local demand and local supply into balance; if the plans bear fruit, today's most popular destination countries can expect to receive fewer students from those countries in future. Other countries may opt not to try to meet every demand within local tertiary education systems. They may judge that it is more cost-efficient to focus their own limited resources in the subject fields and at the levels that have the biggest "mass appeal" locally, and help their residents to go overseas for more specialized and higher-level education and training.

However, we do not believe that the reason that outbound numbers grew faster than local numbers in the U.S. or Australia is because these countries failed to give their populations what they want by way of tertiary opportunities. These two countries, with their diversified, flexible, high-quality systems, together attract more than 25 percent of the world's internationally mobile tertiary students. Both countries have far higher numbers of international students coming in than local students going out; in 2009, according to figures from *Project Atlas*, the ratio was 2.6:1 for the U.S. and 22.3:1 for Australia. However, both countries have strong traditions of internationalization and international academic cooperation.

This brings us to the second big "push factor"—young people wish to study abroad to broaden cultural and intellectual horizons and improve job prospects. As OECD noted in *Education at a Glance 2010*:

> Globally oriented firms seek internationally-competent workers who speak foreign languages and have the intercultural skills needed to successfully interact with international partners. Governments as well as individuals are looking to higher education to broaden students' horizons and help them to better understand the world's languages, cultures and business methods. One way for students to expand their knowledge of other societies and languages, and hence leverage their labour market prospects, is to study in tertiary education institutions in countries other than their own. Several OECD governments have set up schemes and policies to promote mobility as a means of fostering intercultural contacts and building social networks for the future. This intention is especially clear in countries of the European Union that participate in the Bologna process aiming to reach a benchmark of 20% of all graduating students with a study or training period abroad by 2020 (p. 310).

The longstanding academic cooperation and exchange programs that exist in the United States have a similar rationale.

Learning more about another culture and making friends with people in another society has always interested adventurous young people. In cases where countries offer mobility and exchange schemes that support them in doing this, the opportunities are enthusiastically taken up. But as OECD indicates, the prospect of improving one's future job prospects and marketability to employers has become even more important in recent years. In a world where the job market is becoming increasingly globalized and competitive, ambitious young people need an edge over the competition. A second working language can give them that edge—particularly if that language is English—as can experience of another national system and (in professions) the necessary qualifications to practice in another system. Gaining internationally recognized qualifications or completing specialized education or training abroad can also give them an edge, particularly if these are not available to others who rely on their own country's tertiary system. Education systems in many countries, particularly in Central Asia and the Arab states, focus on imparting subject knowledge that may soon become out-of-date and may not also impart the skills required to apply that knowledge and "learn to learn" more in the future. For students from these countries in particular, gaining such skills through study overseas will give them an edge.

We have identified a third push factor from looking at mobility for all educational purposes, including non-tertiary mobility. Some young people study abroad to position themselves for the next stage: education or work. This aspect receives little attention in most other analyses, probably because it is obscured by the lack of comparative data on non-tertiary mobility. Our work in this regard benefitted from access to data for all categories of U.S. Exchange Visitor. In the U.S. country study in part II we observe that the countries ranking high for participation in the exchange visitor scheme for secondary school students tend also to rank high in the exchange visitor scheme for undergraduates, which is not surprising because U.S. secondary schooling may be useful preparation for entering a U.S. university. We note that 11 of the top 20 countries in table II.11 (Secondary School students) also rank in the top 20 table for Exchange Visitor Undergraduate students in table II.12. These places are China, Germany, France, South Korea, Mexico, Japan, Spain, Thailand, Sweden, Taiwan, Italy, and Brazil. The association is particularly true of Asian countries. Of the six Asian countries in table II.11, only Vietnam is missing from the Exchange Visitor Undergraduates' top 20, coming in 23rd. However, Vietnam ranks 9th in the top 20 for all international University and College Students (table II.2).

In a 2008 article, "Korea: The early study abroad trend," author Phuong Ly confirmed that "a growing number of South Korean students are going to English-speaking countries as teenagers in hopes of gaining entry to [U.S.] universities," and incidentally to escape the rigors of the Korean school system. The article notes that this "trend began to take off after 2000 as the Korean middle class grew and the education system became more competitive. More than 20,000 such students left Korea in 2003 and 2004, according to a study from the Korean Educational Development Institute" (Ly, 2008). By 2008, of the 576 Korean undergraduates registered at one American university featured in the article, 60 percent had graduated from U.S. high schools. Even this figure could understate Korean numbers, since some "early study abroad" students obtain a green card or U.S. citizenship and do not register as international students. Similarly, World Education Services reported in their July/August 2010 newsletter that growing numbers of young Vietnamese are enrolling in private U.S. boarding schools with the goal of attending a U.S. university or college.

The same "positioning" phenomenon can be seen at higher levels of education—for example, by studying the associations between the top 20 countries of origin for mobile students in the U.S. undertaking undergraduate and graduate study (see table II.3 for all college and university students, tables II.12 and II.13 for Exchange Visitors only); and between these origin country rankings for graduate study and the origin rankings for professors, teachers, researchers, and scholars in the U.S. (tables 3.7 and 3.9 in chapter 3; tables II.15–17 in part II). "Positioning" is not unique to the U.S.: for example, in 2007 Universities UK published *Talent Wars: The International Market for Academic Staff*, highlighting the extent to which former international students are recruited to fill researcher and other academic posts in the UK.

We do not have the data to track associations between study abroad and taking up employment in the country of study, but we believe that these could be very strong, particularly in developed countries that combine open labor markets with reasonable readiness to grant work permits to highly educated applicants.

Why students may not move: Anti-push factors

Some young people who believe they would benefit from study abroad may be deterred by various obstacles, including financial impediments and travel or visa difficulties, as well as personal or family constraints.

The latest EUROSTUDENT report (2008), which contains a wealth of data about the tertiary study experiences and future plans of young Europeans, sheds light on financial impediments. European countries have agreed as a policy objective that at least 20 percent of all graduates should have had study-related experiences in a foreign country before they enter the labor market. Accordingly, the EUROSTUDENT report has a big section on internationalization and mobility, based on surveys of young people in 20 countries (France, Germany, Spain, Portugal, Italy, Ireland, the Netherlands, Norway, Sweden, Finland, Estonia, Latvia, Lithuania, Czech Republic, Slovakia, Slovenia, Romania, Bulgaria, and Turkey). The dataset captures students who enroll in university courses, participate in work placements, or undertake language courses abroad, so long as they return to their own country afterwards. Those who study abroad are not asked why they decided to do so, unfortunately, but tertiary students who do not study abroad are asked why not. The 2008 survey grouped the answers from these "immobile students" into five main reasons; students could give more than one reason. Fifty-seven percent of students cited "financial insecurities"; 49 percent "insufficient support of mobility in home country" (linked with financial insecurity because students generally understood "support" to mean financial support); 48 percent "lack of individual motivation"; 24 percent "insufficient support of mobility in host country"; and 23 percent "lack of language competency."

Analysis of responses from individual countries showed some differences from this overall picture. Financial insecurity was cited as an obstacle to mobility for particularly large numbers of students in Turkey and Estonia, over 80 percent in both cases. This is understandable in Turkey, the only country where mobile students were 100 percent self-supported, but puzzling in Estonia, where students met only 30 percent of the costs themselves, lower than in any other survey country (public funds supported 53 percent of the cost of foreign study in Estonia). Other countries whose immobile students had greater concerns about finances than the European average were Slovakia, Germany, the Czech Republic, and Spain, whereas less than 40 percent of students from Austria, Bulgaria, and the Netherlands and less than 30 percent of Italians cited financial insecurity as a reason for not studying abroad. The EUROSTUDENT report noted that "Students with an unfavorable socio-economic background perceive this [financial insecurity] to be more of an obstacle than their more privileged counterparts." It concluded that "Financial support and schemes that make [mobility] plans appear feasible are the most decisive instruments by which a positive individual decision can be influenced"—and that the information and support has to be offered by or in the home country.

Potential non-financial obstacles to mobility include difficulties getting a visa in the destination country. Countries rarely intend to cause visa difficulties for bona fide students or scholars, but such difficulties can nonetheless arise. The UK, for example, is making immigration procedures more complex and protracted for bona fide students as an unintended result of efforts to crack down on "bogus students." Also, in some much-publicized recent cases, the general immigration cap the UK introduced this year, combined with a new points-based system that requires applicants for entry to demonstrate a previous salary of at least £25,000, has prevented top research universities from recruiting highly talented ex-Ph.D. students from abroad into research posts because their Ph.D. stipends were below the salary threshold.

Another possible obstacle may be getting permission or travel documents from the home country to go and study abroad. For example, according to a student from Turkmenistan writing in August 2009, "Hundreds of Turkmen students still cannot leave the country in pursuit of education abroad. For nearly a month students have been having problems since the implementation of new rules [meaning] one can only exit the country in pursuit of higher education overseas with the approval of education ministry and state immigration service. The students learned the hard way about the new rule when border officials rejected them at Ashgabat airport. The officials claimed the students didn't have a certificate bearing the national emblem… However, not everybody can get the certificate. Students intending to go to state universities have few problems, but those intending to study in private universities have their requests turned down. They are also reproached for being unpatriotic and almost traitors" (Orazdurdy, 2009). In response, other students confirmed this account and noted that a similar rule operated in Uzbekistan.

In any country where exit permissions have to be sought, even where permission is generally granted, the process of getting permission forms an obstacle, if only a psychological one. Students may feel doubts and mixed feelings about whether they are doing the right thing for their country—well summed-up by the title of Stacy Bieler's book *"Patriots" or "Traitors"? A History of American-Educated Chinese Students.*

How students decide where to go: Pull factors

We list below 12 "pull factors" that draw internationally mobile students to choose one country rather than another as their study destination. We do not attempt to list these factors in order of importance or pulling power—different factors tip the scale for different individuals—but where a factor seems particularly important to students from certain countries, this will be mentioned. The 12 factors are:

- High-quality study opportunities;
- Specialized study opportunities;
- Teaching in a language mobile students speak or want to learn;
- Traditional links and diasporas;

- Affordable cost;
- Internationally recognized qualifications;
- Good prospects of high returns;
- Post-study career opportunities in destination country;
- Good prospects of successful graduation within a predictable time;
- Effective marketing by destination country/institution;
- Home country support for going there to study; and
- Helpful visa arrangements, for study and for work while studying.

High-quality study opportunities

Many mobile students, particularly those whose personal circumstances allow them a free choice of destination, aspire to study in the countries where the world's best universities—or what they perceive as the world's best universities—are to be found. There are now several world rankings available on the Internet, some including rankings by subject and by region. These, and national rankings published in the destination country such as those in *U.S. News and World Report*, have become extremely influential. It is no coincidence that the two leading destination countries for mobile students—the U.S. and the UK, in that order—are also the countries with the most universities in the top 100 of the best-known world university rankings tables.

The desire to go to the best university they can get into, even at great personal and family cost, is particularly strong among mobile students from China. World Education Services' September 2010 newsletter carried an article by Tom Melcher entitled "How Chinese Families Select Overseas Universities" (2010). These were his key points. (1) Quality is all-important, but Chinese families have their own way of judging it. Students and parents are very brand-aware and heavily influenced by whether they have heard of the institution. Well-known universities include Harvard, Yale, Princeton, Columbia, MIT and Stanford in the U.S., Oxford, Cambridge, and the National University of Singapore elsewhere. Universities that "have been accepting hundreds of Chinese students for years, (such as Iowa State and Hong Kong University) are also well known in China" (Melcher, 2010). (2) "Very few Chinese families look at [universities] in more than one country....Most Chinese families prefer the United States. They generally assume that the education is 'better,' and that it will be easier for their child to find a job back in China" with a U.S. degree (Melcher, 2010). They tend to choose the country first and then look at its universities. (3) When selecting a U.S. university, Chinese families rely on *U.S. News & World Report* rankings, because they believe this to be an official U.S. government publication. They focus on the lists for "National Universities" and "Top Graduate Schools" (the latter even when choosing undergraduate programs), and take much persuading that a lower-ranked institution can ever be a better choice than a higher-ranked one. They rarely know about the World University Rankings produced by private organizations.

(4) Things Chinese parents care about when choosing an institution include how safe their child will be on campus, the demographics of the student body, and the financial aid available for graduate programs. Parents expect the student body to be Caucasian rather than rainbow, without too many other Chinese or Koreans. They dislike institutions with rowdy students or religious affiliations. (5) Things unlikely to influence Chinese families' decisions include the cost of and financial aid available for undergraduate programs: if a Chinese family is wealthy enough to afford an overseas undergraduate education, they are not especially sensitive to price differences here. Nor are they bothered about the institution's size, location, accommodation, or sports and student facilities.

Specialized study opportunities

Under "push factors," we established that many countries have difficulty giving every aspiring student tertiary opportunities in the subject field and at the level that they want. OECD sees signs of increasing specialization in the education programs offered by different countries. At the level of advanced research programs, where the most specialized subjects are offered to the fewest individuals, it clearly makes sense for national systems to concentrate research resources in areas of strength and for students to travel to them if necessary. Most countries have significantly higher incoming student mobility, relative to total enrollments, in advanced research programs than in tertiary Type A programs generally. This is true of major destination countries including the United States, the United Kingdom, New Zealand, Canada, Japan, France, Spain, New Zealand, Switzerland, Belgium, South Korea, and Sweden, and of other countries such as Chile (which offers world-leading research opportunities in astronomy).

Another type of specialization is by subject field. Some countries build reputations as the best place to study and obtain internationally marketable qualifications in particular subjects: for example, Germany and Finland for sciences and engineering; Austria, France, Germany, and Japan for linguistic/cultural studies; and the U.S. and Australia for business and law. Sometimes countries can become magnets for certain studies simply by offering more accessible or employment-enhancing programs than neighbors in the same region—for example, aspiring medics from EU countries that restrict access to medical courses by strict quotas may go to study in EU countries without such restrictions, knowing that once qualified they can practice medicine in any EU country (OECD, 2010, p. 321).

Language

As OECD has observed (2010, p. 315), the language spoken and used in instruction is an essential element in the choice of a foreign country in which to study. In this context, not all languages are equal. More and more, as we said in chapter 1, English is the working language of the global economy. Increasingly, mobile students who are not native English speakers choose to do some or all of their studies in an English-speaking environment. The United States, the United Kingdom, Australia, Canada,

New Zealand, and Ireland can expect to continue to attract students for this reason alone; but other countries are increasingly seeking a share of the market by offering courses taught in English. Within the OECD and its partner countries, Denmark, Finland, the Netherlands, and Sweden offer many programs in English. Flemish Belgium, the Czech Republic, France, Germany, Hungary, Iceland, Japan, South Korea, Norway, Poland, Portugal, Slovakia, Switzerland, and Turkey offer some. Non-OECD countries where some English-taught courses can be found include South Africa, India, China, and Thailand.

Other major sending countries and regions, including Russia and Central and South America, show few signs of going down this route. They may not feel the need, having language advantages of their own. Russia, for example, is still the top destination country for many of its former satellite states, where Russian is still spoken (if less than in times past). Data in OECD's *Education at a Glance 2010* show that in 2008, Russia originated 58,983 mobile students but received 143,303, including 92 percent of mobile students from Belarus, 75 percent of those from Kazakhstan, 56 percent of those from Azerbaijan, 53 percent of those from Tajikistan, 37 percent of those from Kyrgyzstan, and 32 percent of those from Ukraine. According to UNESCO's *Global Statistical Digest 2009,* from 1999–2007 the percentage of mobile students from Latin America and the Caribbean going to the mainly Spanish-speaking countries within the region rose by 12.2 percent, while the percentage going to English-speaking North America fell by 11.7 percent.

Traditional links and diasporas

Students from the former Soviet Union who continue to choose Russia as their destination also exemplify the impact on choices of traditional links. Similarly, students from French-speaking countries around the world gravitate back to France. A common language and academic traditions attract U.S. and UK citizens between the two countries, and explain a certain amount of student mobility around the "old Commonwealth" countries (e.g., the United Kingdom, Australia, New Zealand, Canada). Migration networks explain students' propensity to go where previous generations from their home countries have gone (Turks to Germany, Portuguese to France, Mexicans to the United States). Diasporas explain why students whose families were originally from another country often choose to go back to that country to study (Italian Americans to Italy, Jewish Americans to Israel and many other examples). The Indian government is establishing five universities that will target Indian diaspora students in their marketing and reserve half of all places for them.

Affordable cost

OECD also identifies tuition fees and cost of living in destination countries as important factors (2010, p. 316).

EU countries generally treat each other's students as home students for tuition fee purposes, but Scotland charges students from England more than it charges its own or other EU students, and Ireland imposes a three-year residency condition. Among EU and EEA countries, only Finland, Norway, Sweden, and Iceland charge no tuition fees to either domestic or international students (Finland and Sweden are moving toward introducing fees, which may slow their recent growth in popularity as destinations); only France, Germany, Italy, and Spain charge the same fees to both.

Non-EU international students must pay higher tuition fees than home students in all other EU countries, unless they come from EEA countries to which the European Higher Education Area extends. International students are also charged more in New Zealand (with two exceptions: Australian students and advanced research programs), Australia, Canada, Russia, Turkey, and the United States. Strictly speaking, international students in the U.S. are charged the same as domestic students from outside the state where the educational institution is located, but as most domestic students enroll within their state, international students pay more in practice. In Mexico, most institutions charge the same fees to international and domestic students, but some charge international students more. In South Korea, the position varies between institutions, but most international students pay lower fees.

To work out the full cost of their study abroad, students must also consider the costs of maintaining themselves while studying (living costs can be very high in Northern Europe, North America, Japan, and Australia), bearing in mind the chances of getting part-time work while studying; the costs of getting to and from the destination country; and the offsetting financial aid that may be available, such as scholarships or portable student support from their home government.

The EUROSTUDENT data presented earlier in this chapter illustrates that cost and affordability matter to most mobile students and may well be the clinching factor for some, particularly those from less affluent countries (unless they are part of their country's social elite). High costs will not necessarily deter even the less affluent, if they will be buying outstanding quality or exceptional returns or the study opportunities in question are only available in one place. The key question will be whether similar study opportunities are available for less somewhere else, ideally somewhere nearer to the student's home. We have already mentioned that mobile tertiary students are increasingly choosing to study in other countries within their own regions, as these countries strengthen the quantity, quality, and range of their tertiary offerings. We have also discussed how the market shares of the U.S. and the UK have declined in recent years as competition intensifies from other English-speaking countries, such as Australia and New Zealand, both attractively located for the burgeoning numbers of mobile students from East Asia.

<u>Internationally recognized qualifications, prospects of high returns and post-study career opportunities in destination country</u>

Students' chances of capitalizing on their overseas tertiary education depend, or may depend, on these three pull factors. In a competitive global job market, young people are thinking about marketability at the outset of their careers. Students hope to signal their value to employers through qualifications, so these should be as portable as possible. Consequently, more and more young people look for tertiary study opportunities in systems whose degrees, diplomas, and other credentials (e.g., technical or work-related credentials) are recognized and acceptable around the world. This is partly a question of whether the qualification and the type of institution awarding it are well known and understood, and partly a question of how the qualification compares in level, breadth, challenge, and employer acceptability to other internationally and nationally recognized credentials. Most developed countries and some others have arrangements for mutual recognition of qualifications with other countries, through National Recognition Information Centres (NARICs) that can advise on whether qualifications from different systems are equivalent. The work of NARICs is more straightforward where countries have brigaded their qualifications into national frameworks that can be lined up against the frameworks in other countries. Occasionally, such arrangements are superfluous simply because the qualifications obtained are so well-known and respected: every international employer knows, or thinks they know, the worth of a degree from Harvard Law School, a doctorate from Oxford or Cambridge, a German engineering qualification, or a degree from the École Polytechnique. But for the vast majority of mobile students, internationally recognized and portable qualifications will pay dividends, often justifying the choice of a more expensive destination country or program.

Course costs can also be offset and justified by high returns in future employment. This is not only about recognition of the qualification in other countries where mobile students could seek work afterwards, but also about the ease or difficulty of gaining employment in the country of study after graduation and whether salaries there are high compared with the home country. As OECD has noted (2010, p. 323), Chinese mobile students go mostly to Australia, Canada, France, Germany, Japan, New Zealand, the United Kingdom, and the United States; most of these countries have schemes to facilitate the immigration of international students. Similarly, Indian mobile students have tended to go to Australia, the United Kingdom, and the United States.

<u>Good prospects of successful graduation within a predictable time</u>

This is another factor that well-advised mobile students take into account when working out which destination is most affordable and offers the best returns for their study investment. The longer a course typically takes from start to graduation, the greater the cost to the student and the higher the chances that they will drop out, for academic or financial reasons. In some countries courses are designed to be long, either because that is the national tradition or because first degrees go all the way to master's level.

Countries in and around Europe that are signatories to the Bologna process have committed themselves to adopting a three-cycle process offering mutually recognized bachelor's degrees, master's degrees, and Ph.D.s; however, not all signatory countries have yet achieved this for all their degrees. Russia has hardly started, Germany and Slovenia still have quite a way to go, and Hungary and Austria have some way to go (Rauhvargers et al , 2009). In some countries, courses can take significantly longer than their theoretical length, because students face end-year exams with a high failure rate; those who fail have to repeat the year, without necessarily being given the help they need to succeed next time. Two OECD countries from opposite ends of the spectrum illustrate this. In English universities, students take three-year bachelor's degrees, dropout rates are low, students are rarely asked to repeat years, and graduation rates are high. In Chilean universities, first degrees have a theoretical length of at least 5 years, repeats often add another 2–3 years, dropout is high, and graduation rates low. Other things being equal, the country that can offer mobile students the best prospects of the desired result—graduation—within the shortest time will be the most attractive destination country.

Effective marketing by destination country/institution, home country support for going there to study, helpful visa arrangements

These pull factors need little explanation. Effective marketing can boost the attractions of any destination country or institution and induce mobile students who might not otherwise have considered it to study there. Countries committed to internationalization can encourage their students to study overseas by adopting suitable national policies, such as offering scholarships or grants to outgoing students, allowing them to take domestically available student support with them, participating in regional or bilateral exchange schemes, or minimizing potential obstacles to mobility in other ways. Destination countries can make themselves more attractive and overseas students more welcome through national policies, for example by ensuring that visa arrangements admit individuals for education-related purposes without undue difficulty or bureaucratic process and allow them to work to support themselves while studying.

In chapter 5 we will look at a number of major destination or sending countries and consider the impact of their national policies on mobility for education-related purposes.

Chapter 5
THE IMPACT OF NATIONAL POLICIES

Most countries view international academic mobility and educational exchanges as critical to sharing knowledge, building intellectual capital, and remaining competitive in the global economy. Many countries now have well-developed internationalization strategies that aim to foster mutual understanding and cooperation, attract more overseas students, build university linkages, develop joint research programs, and learn from other countries' experiences.

This chapter looks at the national policies of 15 of the top destination and sending countries for internationally mobile tertiary students, and considers the impact of these policies on individuals' decisions on where to study. With permission from the Institute of International Education (IIE), for which we are very grateful, portions of this chapter have been drawn from the IIE/*Project Atlas*® report entitled *Student Mobility and the Internationalization of Higher Education: National Policies and Strategies from Six World Regions—A Project Atlas*® *Report*.

Project Atlas® aims to share accurate and timely data on student mobility at the higher education level, addressing the need for enhanced research on academic migration and comparability of mobility data among leading host and sending countries. As with any data collection effort, there are limitations. Foremost, the definitions of "international student" and "international education" vary across host nations and data providers. For example, some data sources only reflect counts from public institutions, while others collect and report data on students from both public and private institutions. As well, some data sources include students visiting for short-term study, while others only report students studying for a year or more. *Project Atlas* attempts to report harmonized and standardized mobility data to the extent feasible. For the purposes of data reported in *Project Atlas*, international students are defined as those *who undertake all or part of their higher education experience in a country other than their home country* OR *students who travel across a national boundary to a country other than their home country to undertake all or part of their higher education experience.* Offshore students are not included in *Project Atlas* data. More information on each country and individual partner organizations is available on Project Atlas's associated website, the *Atlas of Student Mobility* (www.iie.org/ProjectAtlas), which also highlights country-level data provided by national academic mobility agencies around the world.

By creating a shared image of international mobility, *Project Atlas* brings together an international community of global mobility researchers, publishes comparable data on internationally mobile students worldwide, and invites other countries to contribute to a shared online resource that provides timely and comprehensive global mobility data. *Project Atlas* was initiated in 2001 with support from the Ford Foundation and is now supported by the Bureau of Educational and Cultural Affairs of the U.S. Department of State. It is a collaboration of 17 partner countries and four research affiliates, including OECD and UNESCO, and seeks to complement the data provided by other data-collection organizations.

We will consider, in this order, three countries from the Americas (USA, Canada, and Mexico); three Asian countries (China, India, and Japan); six European countries (UK, France, Germany, the Netherlands, Spain, and Sweden); two from Oceania (Australia and New Zealand); and one from Africa (South Africa). Conclusions will be drawn at the end of the chapter on policies that help and hinder.

THE AMERICAS

The United States of America

The United States hosts the largest international tertiary student numbers of any country, and had 18.7 percent of the world market in 2008, down from 24.1 percent in 2000 (OECD, 2010). In 2009/10, according to figures from IIE's *Open Doors 2010: Report on International Educational Exchange,* 690,923 international students were enrolled in U.S. universities and colleges. Figure 5.1 shows the countries from which the U.S. received the most tertiary students.

Numbers of incoming international students have increased every year since 1995/6, but the latest figures from IIE's *Open Doors 2010* show that the growth is slowing down. Enrollments in 2009/10 were just 2.9 percent higher than in 2008/9, following increases of 7 percent or more in the previous two years. Though numbers from China grew by nearly 30 percent, enabling China to overtake India (which saw growth of just 1.6 percent) as the biggest sender, and Saudi Arabia sent 25 percent more students, enrollments from five of 2008/9's top 10 sending places of origin (South Korea, Canada, Taiwan, Japan, and Mexico) declined. The number of new enrollments rose by 1.3 percent, but mainly because of a 16.4 percent rise in new non-degree students. First enrollments in undergraduate and graduate courses fell, by 3.4 percent and 0.3 percent respectively.

The United States is attractive to international students mainly because of its reputation as a global leader in higher education and training, along with its vast number of accredited higher education institutions, flexible degree programs that cater to all types of students, the work opportunities available post-study, and because courses are taught in English. The country's main disadvantage is its cost as a study location, for both tuition fees (higher for international than for in-state resident students) and living expenses.

FIGURE 5.1: PLACES OF ORIGIN OF INTERNATIONAL STUDENTS ENROLLED IN THE UNITED STATES, 2010

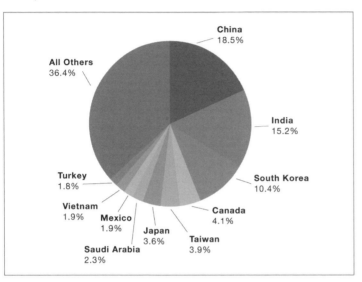

Source: *Open Doors 2010*

In 2008/9, 260,327 U.S. students studied abroad for academic credit, including those on short-term exchanges—a 0.8 percent fall from 2007/8's record high of 262,416 (Chow & Bhandari, 2010). Figure 5.2 shows where they went. Despite the overall fall, the number going to China rose by 4 percent, and some less traditional destinations saw dramatic increases, including Peru (32 percent), South Korea (29 percent), Chile (28 percent), Denmark (21 percent), and Argentina (15 percent).

FIGURE 5.2: DESTINATIONS OF U.S. STUDENTS ENROLLED ABROAD FOR ACADEMIC CREDIT, 2008/9

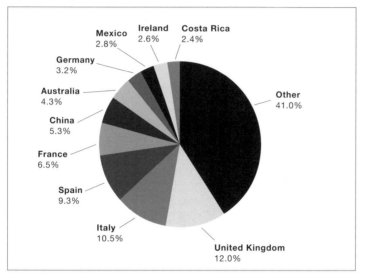

Mexico 2.8%
Ireland 2.6%
Costa Rica 2.4%
Germany 3.2%
Australia 4.3%
China 5.3%
France 6.5%
Spain 9.3%
Italy 10.5%
United Kingdom 12.0%
Other 41.0%

Source: Open Doors 2010

U.S. internationalization policies

Though the U.S. government has no single national policy setting out its international education strategy, it has made strong efforts to keep America's doors open and welcoming to international students. The government shows its commitment to internationalization by running numerous international exchange programs under the auspices of the U.S. Department of State, Department of Education, Department of Defense, and Agency for International Development (USAID), among others. One example is the flagship Fulbright Program, one of the largest federally-funded programs, which includes national government-supported scholarship and fellowship funding for students, educators, and professionals. The funding enables them to engage in international educational exchange opportunities at the graduate and post-doctoral level. Every year the Fulbright Program supports almost 8,000 U.S. and international students and scholars for study outside their home country. Also seen as a vehicle for building mutual understanding, the Fulbright Program includes leadership initiatives to augment the sponsored academic and professional programs. The Fulbright Program has expanded in recent years to additional countries while also addressing language learning needs, for example through the Fulbright English Teaching Assistantship and Foreign Language Teaching Assistantship grants.

U.S. government entities and NGOs also support the internationalization efforts of over 4,000 accredited higher education institutions in the U.S., encouraging the institutions themselves to participate in the exchange and mobility programs and involve their counterparts overseas.

Recent changes to visa regulations have allowed international students to stay in the country for an extended period of time for Optional Practical Training (OPT), allowing up to 29 months for graduates in STEM fields to stay and work in the U.S. after completing their degree. Consular offices have also streamlined student visa processing for applications, particularly in key sending countries such as China and India, by employing additional staff, expanding office hours, and posting on their websites timely updates on waiting times for interviews and appointments.

Overseas students are encouraged to come to the U.S. by EducationUSA, a global network of Advisers supported by the U.S. Department of State's Bureau of Educational and Cultural Affairs. The Advisers provide comprehensive and impartial information on all accredited U.S. higher education institutions. EducationUSA has over 400 advising offices in 169 countries around the world. Advisers are experts on the educational system where they are based, and know about local universities and high schools; this also enables them to help U.S. educational institutions explore opportunities to expand study abroad programs for U.S. students.

A number of U.S. states have active state and/or regional consortia designed to promote their states as destinations for international students. With brands like *Destination Indiana*, *Discover Ohio*, and *One Big Campus* (for the Philadelphia area), states and regions are taking steps to internationalize their institutions' enrollments. Many campuses have ramped up their recruitment of international students over the past decade. Some have established "gateway offices" abroad to provide information on the application procedure and study in the U.S. Institutions are also focusing on improving the international student experience once they arrive, and in some cases, waiving higher out-of-state tuition fees.

U.S. government and institutional goals for study abroad are driven by the need to create more globally-informed citizens, increase expertise in key foreign languages, and prepare citizens for engagement and active participation in a globalized society. The U.S. gives eligible students the same access to Federal Student Aid (loans and Pell Grants) whether they study abroad or at home: few other countries do this. The U.S. Department of State has played a key role in promoting study abroad for U.S. students and diversifying the range of students who participate in terms of backgrounds, destinations, and languages. A number of government-supported nationally-competitive scholarship and fellowship programs help achieve these goals and promote greater diversity and access for groups and academic disciplines that have been underrepresented in the past. Historically, large percentages of the U.S. students studying abroad for academic credit have been Caucasian, female, and pursuing a degree in the humanities or liberal arts. Gradually, this is changing. In addition, more U.S. students are now studying abroad in nontraditional destinations such as the Middle East and Africa.

Among the nationally-supported programs that are encouraging more U.S. citizens to study abroad are the Benjamin A. Gilman Scholarship Program, sponsored by the Bureau of Educational and Cultural Affairs, which provides grants to support U.S. students with limited financial means who would not otherwise have the chance to study abroad at the undergraduate level. Over 2,300 of these scholarships will be awarded in 2010/11, over 60 percent of them to minority students.

Having citizens who are more proficient in the world's languages is also recognized as critical to U.S. national interests. With funding from the National Security Education Program, the David L. Boren Scholarships and Fellowships provide over 230 grants each year to undergraduate and graduate students who wish to study strategically important languages in 50 countries across Africa, Asia, Central and Eastern Europe, Eurasia, Latin America, and the Middle East.

Canada

According to OECD (2010), there were 185,399 foreign tertiary students in Canada in 2007, giving the country 5.5 percent of the world market (up from 4.8 percent in 2000). About half of these foreign students were true "international students" who had come from overseas to study (author's calculations based on OECD, 2010, Table C2.1, which shows both categories as a percentage of Canada's total tertiary enrollment). Among Canada's attractions as a destination—apart from courses taught in English or, in some provinces, French—is the strength of its higher education system in sciences, agriculture, and engineering, which attracted 32.2 percent of 2007's foreign students, and in advanced research programs, where foreign students made up 38.6 percent of 2007 enrollments (OECD, 2010).

In 2008, 45,157 students from Canada studied in other countries. 44,185 of them went to OECD countries. The greatest numbers by far (29,082) went to the U.S., followed by the UK (5,003), Australia (4,321), and France (1,378) (OECD, 2010).

Figure 5.3 shows the top 10 countries sending international students to Canada in 2009, led by China, with their enrollment shares (Canadian Bureau for International Education [CBIE], 2011).

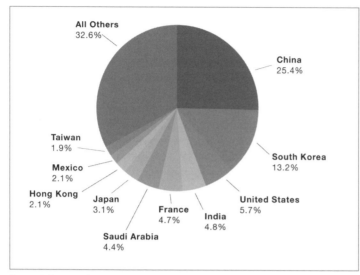

Source: The Canadian Bureau for International Education (CBIE)

Canada's internationalization policies

Canada's educational institutions and associations and its federal and provincial governments are keenly interested in student mobility. The major national organization dedicated exclusively to international education is the Canadian Bureau for International Education (CBIE), which has undertaken major studies of Canadian students abroad and international students' experiences in Canada. While both inbound and outbound mobility are priorities, greater attention has been paid in recent years to attracting international students from other countries.

International student numbers at all levels of education more than doubled in ten years, from 97,336 in 1999 to 196,227 in 2009 (Citizenship and Immigration Canada, 2010). The governments of Canada encourage international students to come to the country on the basis that they make a significant contribution to Canadian society. As Canada evolves from a resource-based to a knowledge-based economy, the best and brightest from around the world can make a significant contribution to the broad knowledge base the country needs to compete globally, as well as diversifying Canadian campuses and increasing the global-mindedness of Canadian students, faculty, and staff. Drawing new international talent into academia and the national labor force is particularly important given Canada's demographics: rising numbers of people retiring and a modest number of young people entering the labor market. The off-campus spending of international students is also economically valuable. International students in Canada can help to fill labor market gaps, both by working off-campus while studying and by taking jobs in skill shortage areas on graduation. Those who return home are a source of future partners in trade, political relations, and global leadership. The Department of Foreign Affairs and International Trade's (DFAIT) International Education and Youth Division is responsible for Canada's foreign policy in the areas of knowledge, learning, and the promotion of Canada as a study and research destination.

For educational institutions, international students represent a rich source of new perspectives and research talent. They also pay higher fees than Canadian students and therefore have a positive impact on an institution's bottom line. A 2009 report commissioned by DFAIT, *The Economic Impact of International Education in Canada*, found that $6.5B annually is contributed to the Canadian economy from international students through tuition, living costs, travel while in Canada, and visits from family. International students in Canada also create 83,000 domestic jobs and contribute $291M in government revenue per annum.

Canada encourages inward student mobility in a number of ways. The first is through helpful policies for visas, immigration, and working while studying. Citizenship and Immigration Canada (CIC) has over the past few years introduced the Off-Campus Work Permit (OCWP) and extended the length of the Post-Graduation Work Permit program (PGWP), as well as making it more widely accessible. CIC has also eased the process for visa applications from international students and reduced the processing times for student visa applications and renewals through an online application system. The OCWP and PGWP have already proved extremely popular. In 2008, 16,000 students were granted OCWP, representing about 40 percent of those eligible; and 18,000 graduates applied for PGWP, up 63 percent from 2007. In addition, the Canadian Experience Class program facilitates international students' migration to Canada by enabling them to apply for permanent residency.

As part of the promotion of Canada as an education destination, DFAIT has targeted nine priority countries from which to increase student mobility—Brazil, China, France, Germany, India, Japan, South Korea, Mexico, and the U.S.—and four priority regions: ASEAN, the Caribbean, the Arabian Gulf, and North Africa. DFAIT's *Education au/in Canada's IMAGINE* is Canada's new international education promotion brand that advertises Canada to prospective international students. A 2009 survey found that 31 percent of South Korean students studying in Canada who saw advertising about Canada as a study destination reported that the advertising influenced them very much, followed by 29 percent of German, Indian, and Japanese students, 26 percent of U.S. students, 25 percent of French students, 24 percent of Mexican students, 20 percent of Brazilian students, and 18 percent of Chinese students.

There are several scholarship programs to attract students from specific regions. On behalf of DFAIT, CBIE administers scholarships to promote mobility within the Americas, including the Emerging Leaders in the Americas Program, the Canada-Chile Leadership Program, and the Canada-CARICOM Leadership Program. Other programs are offered for students from Commonwealth countries, and from Asia, Africa, and Europe. CBIE hosts an Annual Conference focused on mobility, and in October 2010 co-hosted the inaugural Conference of the Americas on International Education in Calgary, Alberta. CBIE also provides research and statistics on issues such as how to improve international students' experience. Over the coming years, Canada intends to improve and expand scholarships; achieve smoother processing of study permits and work permits; and improve professional development for international educators.

The governments of Canada also promote study abroad for domestic students, to encourage increased language capability, cultural sensitivity and an expanded view of the world, and to build a future network of internationalized intellectuals. All of this helps to ensure that Canadians are global citizens and can cooperate as well as compete internationally.

Mexico

Mexico's outbound student numbers are much greater than its incoming numbers. 28,627 tertiary students were enrolled overseas in 2008, of whom 26,657 went to other OECD countries. Over half (14,853) went to the U.S., followed by Spain (3,551), Canada (1,760), France (1,751), Germany (1380), and the UK (1,303) (OECD, 2010).

There were 2,880 international tertiary students in Mexico in 2007 (National Association of Universities and Higher Education Institutions [ANUIES], 2011). Figure 5.4 shows the top 10 places they came from, led by the U.S., the destination for more than one in three.

FIGURE 5.4: PLACES OF ORIGIN OF INTERNATIONAL STUDENTS IN MEXICO, 2007

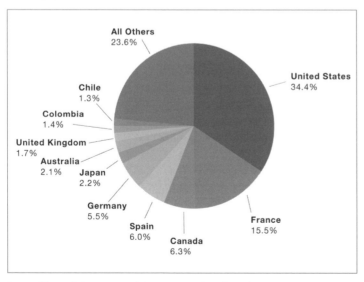

Source: National Association of Universities and Higher Education Institutions (ANUIES)

Mexico's internationalization policies

Mexico's government promotes inbound student mobility in order to diversify Mexico's student population and enhance its academic culture. Both inbound and outbound mobility allow students to develop wider cultural perspectives and broaden their understanding of other countries' languages and cultural, economic, and business patterns. Mexican students who study abroad are often graduate-level students who can bring back to Mexico the benefits of high-quality training in priority disciplines and thereby contribute to capacity building and human resource development in Mexico.

Mexico encourages inward mobility in the following practical ways.

- The tertiary system is flexible about recognizing previous courses of study and degrees obtained in other countries.

- Mexico's Department of Foreign Affairs implements a scholarship program for undergraduate and graduate students from Central-South America and the Caribbean.

- The National Council for Science and Technology (CONACYT) runs various initiatives to encourage inward mobility. These include: The National Register of Quality Post-graduate Programs, under which every year universities can have their programs evaluated and certified against a national standard; and The National System of Researchers (SNI), which supports researchers locally with monthly stipends and evaluation-based official recognition.

- The National Immigration Institute (INM) has implemented recent reforms intended to facilitate legal processes for incoming students, including waiving visa fees for international students. However, significant challenges remain for students from some Latin American countries, such as Colombia and Bolivia.

- The National Association of Universities and Higher Education Institutions (ANUIES) promotes short-term student and faculty mobility through exchange programs, especially for researchers and lecturers; develops cooperation programs with international counterparts; and manages the distribution of information about grants, academic opportunities, and scholarships.

- ANUIES has also developed surveys to study the development of academic and student mobility programs, particularly those involving short-term exchanges; and has tried to collect and maintain data on student mobility, which has not been done before in Mexico (the only OECD member country not to report incoming international mobility figures to OECD).

Mexico, through CONACYT, also encourages outbound student mobility by funding an international scholarship program to support Ph.D. and Master's level students to study abroad. Priority is given to science and technology areas of study, including biotechnology, medicine, energy, environment, manufacturing technologies, materials, nanotechnology, information technology, telecommunications, and applied mathematics.

ASIA

China

According to OECD, China exports more students for tertiary education than any other country—510,842 enrolled overseas in 2008 (OECD, 2010, Table C2.7). Of these outgoing Chinese students, 446,290 went to OECD member or partner countries, among which the 10 most popular destinations were the U.S. (110,246), Japan (77,916), Australia (57,596), the UK (45,356), Canada (36,275), South Korea (30,552), Germany (25,479), France (20,852), New Zealand (13,767), and Russia (9,187).

By 2008 China had also become an important destination country, ranking 14th in the world and hosting 1.5 percent of the world's mobile tertiary students. China is fast becoming a hub for regional and global mobility. The country's growth and strength as a world economic power are persuading more and more students that they should learn to speak Mandarin Chinese and understand Chinese society and culture, so as to do business with the country and its people in the future. According to figures from the China Scholarship Council (CSC) (2011) based on returns from higher education institutions, there were 238,184 foreign higher education students in China in 2009 (an increase of 6.6 percent over 2008), attending 610 different institutions in 31 provinces, autonomous regions, and municipalities. Figure 5.5 shows the top 10 countries for sending their students to China in 2009. More than one in four foreign students comes from South Korea.

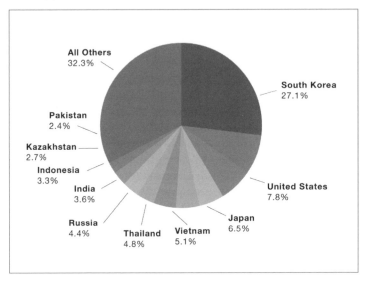

Source: China Scholarship Council (CSC)

China's internationalization policies

Through its scholarship and educational policy arm, the CSC, the Chinese govern-ment supports inbound and outbound mobility in order to promote Chinese culture; fosters people-to-people communications between foreign countries and China; enhances the competitiveness and internationalization of Chinese higher education; stimulates Sino-foreign educational exchanges and scientific research collaborations; and cultivates creative and international talent through the overseas education of Chinese students and scholars.

CSC works in a number of ways to support outbound Chinese student mobility. A major activity involves administering national scholarship programs. CSC provides 12,000 scholarships annually to Chinese citizens for study overseas. There is also a spe-cial program that provides state scholarships to high-achieving self-financed students studying abroad through a competitive selection process. Since the program began in 2003, over 1,400 Chinese students have been awarded these scholarships. By November 2009, a total of 58,419 Chinese citizens had been granted government scholarships to study abroad. Their average return rate is 97 percent. Many scholars who return after an overseas study experience have played a key role in various fields toward national capacity building in China. Latterly, China has been placing increas-ing emphasis on outgoing mobility within the Asian region, which facilitates the mutual recognition of degrees, certificates, and academic credits. The Chinese government is making strides to send more Chinese students to higher education institutions within Asia, with the goal of improving regional economic development, social cohesion, and stability.

For inbound international students, China now represents one of the top destinations in Asia. The Chinese government is keen to promote China as a leading study abroad destination. As with outbound mobility funding programs, the CSC is responsible for overseeing government and other sponsored scholarships for international students to study at Chinese universities. Approximately 20,000 scholarships are granted annually to international students to further their education in China. Since 2008, all the universities in 'Project 985'—which aims to found a cadre of world-class research universities—have been allowed to act independently in recruiting and granting government scholarships to foreign students interested in graduate studies in China. Nine provinces and autonomous regions have been given the same independent authority in relation to foreign graduate students from neighboring countries. And since 2002, CSC has organized "China's Higher Education" exhibitions in more than 20 world countries and regions; these attract large numbers of interested potential students.

Over the next ten years, China intends to continue its policy of boosting both inward and outbound mobility. The country will continue to educate a considerable number of students, scholars and professionals overseas, so that they can make an enhanced contribution to the Chinese economy and society on return. It will also continue to boost the numbers of international students studying in China and increase the number of Chinese government scholarships offered to them, so as to improve the level of China's engagement in global educational cooperation and exchanges. China's latest national educational plan includes an aim of having 500,000 international students enrolled by 2020, and becoming Asia's top destination country for international students ("China wants to have a half million international students in 10 years." September 28, 2010).

India

India has a long history of sending students abroad for higher education, with the number of outbound students having increased exponentially over the last 40 years. Indians comprise the second largest group of the world's mobile student population; only China exports more. In 2008 India's outgoing student numbers reached 184,801, of whom only 11,687 went to non-OECD countries (OECD 2010). By far the most popular OECD member destination for Indian students in 2008 was the U.S. with 94,664, followed by Australia with 26,664, the UK with 25,901, Canada with 10,357, New Zealand with 5,426, Russia with 4,314, Germany with 3,644, and France with 1,038.

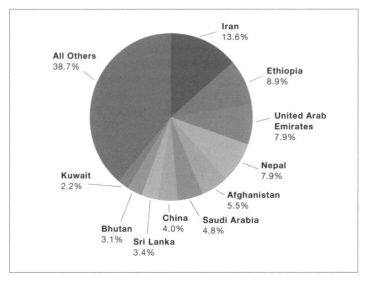

Source: Association of Indian Universities (AIU)

India has not been among the leading destinations, probably due to the same issues of higher education sector quality and capacity that lead so many young Indians to seek educational opportunities elsewhere. However, students from 195 countries come to India for undergraduate, graduate, and research programs. Figure 5.6 shows where they come from (Association of Indian Universities [AIU], 2011).

India's internationalization policy

India hopes to increase its attractiveness as an educational destination for international students in the coming years. The economic boom in India over the last two decades, combined with the priority the fast-growing Indian middle class places on quality educational opportunities for their children, has created a national imperative to improve the capacity of the education sector and make supply match demand.

Currently composed of 532 universities and 25,951 colleges and enrolling 14 million students, the Indian higher education sector is one of the largest in the world, but the demands on it still far exceed the available supply. Indian Government Minister Kapil Sibal announced recently that the central government is looking to add 1,000 more universities and 30 million more students to higher education by 2020 (World Education Services newsletter, Dec. 2010).

Improving the educational system is a high priority for the government, which has introduced a number of measures to internationalize the higher education sector, including the following:

- In 2004/05 the University Grants Commission (UGC) implemented a coordination system for promoting Indian higher education overseas, though it has seen limited success in increasing recruitments.

- EdCil, the coordinating agency for admitting international students, recruits around 1,000 students a year, as does the Indian Council for Cultural Relations, the government's public diplomacy division.

- In 2005, the government formed the National Knowledge Commission (NKC) to advise the Prime Minister on policies to improve the education sector, resulting in a number of policy recommendations.

- The government has recently taken steps to encourage inbound student mobility by streamlining the visa process and allowing for students to receive multi-entry visas when engaging in long-term courses.

- In May 2009, universities were directed to increase information and support for international students, through launching websites, providing orientation sessions, and increasing monitoring services for overseas students in India.

- The government has plans to establish five universities that will reserve half of their places specifically for Indian diaspora students.

- The Foreign Educational Institutions (Regulation of Entry and Operations) Bill 2010 is intended to open up the educational landscape to more partnerships and collaborative arrangements with foreign providers. The Bill would eliminate the present rules that require foreign providers to partner with Indian institutions and prevent them from conferring their own degrees in India. These changes should help attract new institutions and investment from abroad, encourage international collaborations and teacher and researcher exchange between overseas and domestic institutions, and so improve the choice of high-quality tertiary programs in India, both for non-mobile Indian students and for international students.

The Association of Indian Universities (AIU) has supported internationalization efforts in a variety of ways, including the following:

- AIU has signed Memorandums of Understanding (MOUs) with Australia, Egypt, Germany, Russia, and Sri Lanka, which allow for reciprocal recognition of degrees awarded by accredited institutions in one as the basis for admissions into higher education institutions in the other.

- AIU also publishes the *Universities Handbook,* which contains important information on affiliated institutions' accreditation status, course offerings, admissions procedures, and academic staff.

- To facilitate outbound mobility and strengthen research capacity in the country, AIU coordinates National Research Conventions that link international host institutions with promising young Indian students interested in pursuing research careers. The aim is to identify students with research promise while simultaneously promoting the need for talented researchers in the country. Students selected through these conventions are potentially eligible for research fellowships at universities in countries such as Canada, Germany, and the Netherlands.

Japan

In 2009, Japan hosted 132,720 international students. Figure 5.7 shows where those international students came from—more than half are from just one country, China (Japan Student Services Organization [JASSO], 2011).

According to OECD (2010), the country's 2008 figure of 126,568 incoming foreign tertiary students gave it a 3.8 percent share of the world market, up 0.4 percent since 2000 and eighth in the world. About 9 in 10 of these foreign students were international students (OECD, 2010).

In 2008, 52,849 Japanese students were enrolled in other countries in tertiary education courses lasting at least a year (OECD 2010). Only 1,201 went to non-OECD countries. The most popular destination by far for Japanese students abroad was the U.S. (34,010), followed by the UK (4,465), Australia (2,974), Germany (2,234), Canada (2,169), France (1,908), South Korea (1,062), and New Zealand (1,051). Also in 2008, Japanese tertiary institutions enrolled 126,568 international students and had 3.8 percent of the world market.

FIGURE 5.7: PLACES OF ORIGIN OF INTERNATIONAL STUDENTS IN JAPAN, 2009

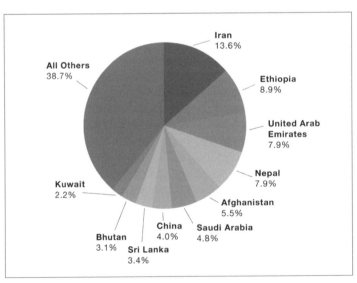

Source: Japan Student Services Organization (JASSO)

Japan's internationalization policies

The Japanese government is keenly interested in increasing both inbound and outbound student mobility. Though reduced numbers of Japanese students have pursued education abroad in recent years, this has been mainly due to a declining young population. In an effort to develop its higher education system as a hub for global international students and to support the exchange of students, particularly within the region, the government has recently implemented a number of key initiatives.

In July 2009, the government announced the "300,000 International Students Plan," which aims to increase Japan's international student population to 300,000 students by 2020.

The first component of the plan involves proactive, coordinated dissemination of information about Japanese culture and higher education. Key stakeholders abroad such as Japan's consulates, embassies, and branch campuses of universities are being encouraged to work together to provide comprehensive information on studying in Japan to potential international students. The number of language education bases to promote Japanese language acquisition abroad will also be increased.

The plan's second component focuses on streamlining various processes for international students to ease their entry into the country, from the initial application process through visa and immigration procedures to enrollment. The plan asks institutions to give potential students better information about Japanese admissions requirements, particularly entrance exams, and aims to improve the standard admission test for non-Japanese students.

As the third major component of the plan, the Ministry of Education, Culture, Sports, Science, and Technology (MEXT) launched the "Project for Establishing Core Universities for Internationalization," also known as the Global 30 Program.[1] The project involves 30 Japanese universities, of which 13 have been selected. The mission of the selected universities is to increase the number of both inbound and outbound students, by revising admissions processes, establishing overseas offices to bolster recruitment, making fall (autumn) entry easier, increasing the number of degree programs offered solely in English while also providing opportunities for Japanese language and cultural instruction, and increasing the number of foreign teachers. To support these internationalization goals, the selected universities were promised increased government funding with which to recruit 3,000-8,000 international students over five years. The government also named seven countries where international offices will be established, each affiliated with one of the 13 universities. These will be Bonn, Germany (Waseda University); Cairo, Egypt (Kyushu University); Hanoi, Vietnam (Kyoto University); Hyderabad, India (The University of Tokyo); Moscow and Novosibirsk, Russia (Tohoku University); New Delhi, India (Ritsumeikan University); Tashkent, Uzbekistan (Nagoya University); and Tunis, Tunisia (University of Tsukuba).

The fourth component of the plan centers on improving support services for international students within the higher education system. A primary focus is on increasing the accommodation options available to international students through building more dormitories and providing assistance with securing off-campus housing. Other forms of support targeted at self-funded international students include governmental and merit-based scholarships and financial counselling services.

The plan's final component involves integrating international students into Japanese society through employment in Japan after they complete their studies. The government, universities, and private industry have all been asked to take specific measures to increase international students' job prospects. Universities have been instructed to improve careers services. The government will consider immigration reforms to extend the current maximum time international students are allowed to stay in the country after finishing their studies. Companies have been encouraged to develop policies to accept more international graduates into employment.

The Japanese government remains keen to foster exchange partnerships within the region, particularly through trilateral cooperation with China and South Korea. In April 2010, the "Japan-China-Korea Committee for Promoting Exchange and Cooperation among Universities" met in Tokyo, and agreed to set up the "CAMPUS Asia" project. This aims to develop increased intra-regional student mobility through agreed approaches to quality assurance, credit transfer, grading and assessment policies, and university evaluation.

In support of these national initiatives, the Japanese Student Services Organization (JASSO) provides services to students and higher education institutions to support student mobility. JASSO:

- serves as an information resource for potential international students and Japanese students interested in studying abroad;

- organizes education fairs overseas as well as college guidance fairs and study abroad fairs in Japan;

- provides scholarships and financial services under the higher education Student Exchange Support Program, for both inbound and outbound mobility, whether for long-term studies or short-term exchanges;

- co-manages the Japan-East Asia Network of Exchange for Students and Youths (JENESYS), established by the government in 2007 to provide a variety of exchange opportunities for students from the region to visit Japan, thereby promoting mutual understanding and fostering positive regard for Japan among the youth of Asia;

- provides student services to international students, from the initial stages of admission to Japanese universities, through their enrollment in academic programs, and as alumni;

- facilitates the Examination for Japanese University Admission for International Students (EJU), the standard admission test for non-Japanese candidates;

- provides Japanese language education for students interested in higher education in Japan;

- manages accommodation and helps universities to lease accommodation for international students; and

- follows up former international students in Japan to support them in their future careers, offering research guidance, fellowships, and job hunting seminars. An e-mail newsletter, the "Japan Alumni eNews," allows former international students to network and keep them connected to their educational experience in Japan.

EUROPE

United Kingdom

The UK hosts the second largest numbers of international tertiary students of any country (the U.S. hosts the largest). In 2008, 335,870 international students, or 10 percent of the world market, were enrolled in UK tertiary institutions—though, like the U.S., Germany and others, the UK has seen its market share decline in recent years. International students accounted for 14.7 percent of all tertiary enrollment (only Australia had a higher percentage) and 42 percent of all enrollment on advanced research programs (only Switzerland, with 46 percent, had a higher percentage) (OECD, 2010). In addition, in recent years around 700,000 international students a year have come to the UK for sub-tertiary courses, 100,000 of them to attend further education colleges and 600,000 of them to learn English.

Figure 5.8 identifies the 10 countries that sent the most tertiary students to the UK in 2009 (British Council, 2011), and also shows that those top 10 countries account for only 51 percent of the incoming student total. The UK draws in international students from almost everywhere in the world, attracting international students for much the same reasons as the U.S. The higher education system has an excellent reputation worldwide, second only to that of the U.S.; and if world ranking results were adjusted for population size, the UK would have more universities in the top 100. The UK can offer international students a wide range of flexible education and training programs at, above and below first degree level, in universities, higher education colleges and further education colleges, all leading to recognized qualifications with worldwide recognition. The chances of graduation within a relatively short and predictable time are very good, with most bachelor's degrees taking three years, most master's degrees one year, and drop-out generally low; this remains a big attraction for students from other EU countries where things are different. And, of course, courses are taught in English. However, the UK is expensive for non-EU international students, with high tuition fees and high living costs.

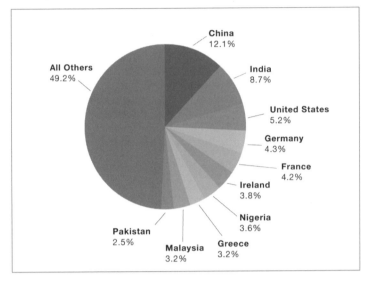

Source: HESA data provided by the British Council

The numbers of UK students traveling abroad for tertiary study of a year or more are much lower than the numbers coming in from other countries: 28,712 in 2008, putting the UK 25th in the list of exporting countries (OECD, 2010). The most popular destinations for UK students in 2008 were the U.S. (8,376), New Zealand (4,001), France (2,519), Canada (2,518), Germany (1,723), Australia (1,696), and Ireland (1,421).

The UK's internationalization policies

The UK government changed in 2010, but Education Ministers in the new government are at least as committed as their predecessors to internationalization and learning from the experience of other countries. In the UK there is general agreement that international student mobility offers the opportunity to build more connections between individuals across countries through educational and cultural exchange, equipping a new generation with the skills and understanding they will need to rise to global challenges.

International tertiary students coming to the UK are seen as contributing immeasurably to the intellectual vitality of UK education, making a key contribution to the UK's research capacity and its standing in the globalized knowledge economy, particularly in the scientific and technical fields that struggle to attract enough domestic students. The presence of international students on British campuses also helps to ensure that a wider range of courses is available for UK students. They provide a driver to maintain high quality course provision as UK universities compete in an increasingly competitive market to attract them; they enrich the diversity of campuses and communities and help to broaden the outlook and understanding of UK students as they prepare to join a global workplace; and by paying tuition fees equivalent to the full costs of their courses, international students from outside the EU make a major contribution to the continuing viability of the UK higher education system and to the national economy.

Study abroad equips UK students with the vital skills they need to prosper in a global economy as they enter the workforce of their home country and develop their careers. It also sets the stage for greater collaboration and exchange of ideas among the world's best and brightest young minds. Outward mobility can help students to develop academically and personally; to build up their language skills; to grow in understanding of other societies and cultures; and to forge lifelong friendships with overseas counterparts.

Practical policies and initiatives to encourage international students to come to the UK include the following.

- The Prime Minister's Initiative for International Education (PMI), a five-year national strategy to support UK engagement in the global education arena, launched in 2006 and managed by the British Council. This promotes UK higher education and provides a mechanism for education institutions in the UK to link strategically with counterparts overseas. PMI objectives include providing a national brand and communications platform for UK education as both partner and educator; providing information to help international students access UK education opportunities; building the UK's profile as a potential collaborator in international education partnerships, whether they relate to higher, further, or vocational education; enhancing the quality of international students' experience in the UK; and enhancing the employability of international graduate students. However, there are presently no plans to continue this initiative (of the previous Prime Minister) beyond April 2011.

- The work of the British Council, Britain's international cultural relations body, through its network of overseas offices. The British Council represents British education abroad and provides information, guidance, and support to young people interested in studying in the UK— face-to-face via pre-departure briefings or walk-in centers, on the Education UK website, or through publications, marketing, and PR campaigns.

- The work of the UK Council for International Student Affairs (UKCISA), a national advisory body serving the interests of international students in the UK and those who work with them. UKCISA aims to increase support for international education and raise awareness of its values and benefits; promote opportunities for—and identify and work to reduce obstacles and barriers to—greater student mobility; and encourage best practice, professional development, and the highest quality of institutional support for international students in all types and levels of education. UKCISA monitors government policy affecting international students and seeks to influence it in their interests; produces regular electronic and print publications on current legislation, regulations, and resources; delivers advice line services and training; and initiates and encourages relevant research.

- The extensive promotional and partnership activities of Universities UK, of the bodies representing higher and further education colleges, and of the institutions themselves.

- A number of partnership-building projects for specific countries or regions, funded or managed by the British Council. These include International Strategic Partnerships in Research and Education (INSPIRE), to strengthen academic and research partnerships between HE institutions in the UK and in Afghanistan, Bangladesh, Kazakhstan, Pakistan, and Uzbekistan; Development Partnerships in Higher Education (DelPHE), to fund HE institutions working collaboratively on activity linked to development goals in Africa and Asia; the UK–India Education and Research Initiative (UKIERI), a five-year program to improve educational links between India and the UK; and Education Partnerships in Africa (EPA), for English higher and further education institutions wishing to work in partnership with counterparts in sub-Saharan Africa.

- Various scholarship schemes for incoming students, including Fulbright and Chevening. The prestigious Chevening scholarships fund international graduate students wishing to study in the UK for one academic year, though the scheme's Foreign and Commonwealth Office funding is currently under review. Higher education institutions may offer their own scholarships.

There are fewer schemes and initiatives to encourage UK students to study abroad, but these again include scholarship schemes (such as Fulbright) and the Erasmus scheme—mentioned in earlier chapters—which supports student mobility within Europe. The "fee waiver," a government initiative introduced in 1999, ensures that UK students who are studying outside the UK for a year under Erasmus do not have to pay fees to their home institution. As their host institution pays any fee due for the study abroad, these students receive a fee-free year of study—already a strong incentive to outward mobility and likely to become more of an incentive in future (see below). Over 5,500 UK students were eligible to receive this waiver in 2008-09.

Over the next few years, the higher education system in the UK faces huge changes in current arrangements for funding higher and further education institutions and student support, though the changes so far announced mainly affect England, not Scotland, Wales, or Northern Ireland. Essentially, much of the funding burden will switch from the public purse to domestic students, who will have to pay fees twice or three times as high as they pay now. A large proportion of universities' present funding for teaching will be withdrawn; funding at present levels will remain only for teaching priority science and technology subjects and for research. The funding and student support changes will apply equally to EU students at English higher education institutions. In principle, these changes should not affect non-EU international students, who already pay full-cost fees averaging over £10,000 a year (total value £2.2 billion in 2008/9), and will find themselves welcomed even more warmly by higher education institutions in the future (Partridge, December 23, 2010). In practice, such far-reaching changes may have unforeseeable consequences for the UK higher education system.

Immigration and visa arrangements are also changing, in ways that are likely to have consequences for non-EU international students considering study anywhere in the UK. The government is concerned both about high immigration levels generally and about high numbers of people arriving on student visas who either overstay on finishing their studies or never study at all. Until the Government decides on permanent arrangements in April 2011, temporary solutions have included an overall immigration cap and entry quotas for certain categories of entrants. The combined effect has been to keep out of the country several hundred researchers and scholars that British universities wished to take on.

The UK government has promised to fix this problem from April 2011, and has also said that it does not wish to discourage bona fide international students arriving for courses at degree level or above. However, UK education institutions were dismayed by the proposals for revising student visa arrangements published for consultation on December 7, 2010 (UK Border Agency, December 2010). The proposals include: restricting student visas largely to degree-level courses and child students, allowing only Highly Trusted Sponsors (a status for which only education providers with a proven track record of student retention and visa compliance can qualify—so far, only a third of all existing providers have done so) to offer sub-degree courses to adults from overseas—unless these courses last less than six months, in which case the Student Visitor route is available; requiring all international applicants for student visas to pass an English test, even if they seek entry for an English Language course; allowing students to continue studying in the UK after completing their course only if they prove they are entering a higher level course; closing a main route by which students can stay in the UK and find work after graduation; banning international students from working while studying, except on campus, at weekends, and during vacations; reducing the maximum time that can be spent on work placement while studying; banning students' dependants from working unless they qualify to do so in their own right through another visa route; banning students from bringing dependents with them unless their courses last more than 12 months; and tightening current arrangements for accrediting private educational institutions and allowing them to take international students.

The consultation paper says: "In implementing our proposals we will continue to monitor how our system of student migration compares with key competitor countries to ensure we continue to be attractive to the genuine international students from across the world." However, if these visa changes proceed as planned, it seems likely that at least some students who would otherwise have come to the UK for courses at degree level or above will be discouraged by the restrictions—particularly but not only those on working during and after study—and will go elsewhere. The impact below tertiary level, on numbers of international students undertaking the further education and English language courses that give many their entry route to a UK university, is likely to be devastating. This may well have major consequences for tertiary numbers in future years, as well as for the UK economy.

France

In 2008, according to OECD (2010), France hosted 243,436 foreign tertiary students enrolled on courses of a year or more. These foreign students made up 11.2 percent of France's tertiary enrollment and 39.8 percent of enrollment on advanced research programs. France was the world's fourth most popular destination for internationally mobile students, but with another 2,100 students would have overtaken Germany, which came third—both countries had 7.3 percent of the world market.

However, France's numbers have been growing faster than Germany's in recent years—78 percent between 2000 and 2008, compared to Germany's 31 percent—and according to the figures provided by *CampusFrance* (2011) and DAAD (2011), France had over 278,213 foreign students enrolled in 2009 compared to Germany's 244,776. Though there are differences between *Project Atlas* and OECD definitions, this suggests that when OECD publishes figures for 2009, France may well have overtaken Germany to reach third position in the world. The top 10 sending countries in 2010 are shown in Figure 5.9; but as in the UK, almost half of France's overseas students are from other countries (*CampusFrance*, 2011).

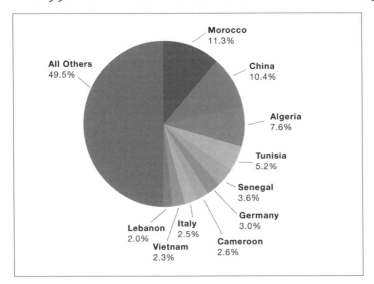

Source: CampusFrance

In 2008, OECD (2010) records that 63,081 French students travelled to other countries for tertiary studies, 62,264 within the OECD and 817 to non-OECD countries. The top 11 countries they went to were Belgium (16,650), the UK (12,685), the U.S. (7,058), Canada (6,325), Germany (5,784), Switzerland (4,690), Spain (1,884), Australia (1,027), Italy (1,013), Portugal (823), and the Netherlands (822).

When comparing France's numbers with those of other countries, it should be borne in mind that—like Germany, but unlike the U.S. and the UK, which came first and second, and Australia, which came quite a close fifth in OECD's destination country rankings for 2008—France does not count international students i.e. those who reside in another country, but foreign students i.e. all those who are not citizens, so may well include some of its own long-term residents in its totals.

France's internationalization policies

The French government conducts active internationalization policies, designed to attract international students to the French higher education sector, to develop relationships between citizens of France and other countries, and to promote the French language abroad. The government has put in place the following measures to support inbound student mobility and the development of international partnerships.

Because higher education is considered to be a public good, the French government meets a large part of its cost, subsidising tuition costs by €10,150 per student per year on average. International students qualify for the same low fees and social benefits as domestic students. These benefits include university housing, rent subsidies, health insurance, student clubs and associations, and discounts on public transportation and cultural events.

A number of national bodies have been set up to support internationalization efforts. *CampusFrance* (set up as *EduFrance* in 1998) promotes French higher education throughout the world, but particularly in Asia, Latin America, the Middle East, Africa, and other European countries. *Égide,* the national body responsible for supporting international students, has been managing international exchange and grant programs for international students and interns taking part in courses in France or abroad for over 45 years. The *Centre National des Oeuvres Universitaires et Scolaires* (CNOUS) is an independent public establishment that manages a network of student social services domestically and internationally, supporting equal opportunity and access to higher education. The services range from housing grants and social and cultural activities, to administering international mobility programs and partnerships.

CampusFrance works in conjunction with higher education institutions to attract international students to higher education in France and assist them at all stages, from initial inquiry to the trip home to their countries of origin. The organization currently has 242 member organizations, including *Grandes Ecoles*, business schools, engineering schools, specialized institutions, and most universities. It has a network of 116 overseas offices and 24 annexes in 89 countries, supervised by the French Embassy in each country. These offices provide counseling and information services to individual students interested in pursuing their studies in France, while promoting French higher education at local institutions. *CampusFrance* staff also help students through the administrative and consular processes prior to their arrival in France. An online application system that can also handle visa request procedures has been set up in nearly 30 countries.

On average, *CampusFrance* organizes promotional events throughout the world each year, which attract around 160,000 visitors. These events, which representatives of French HEIs take part in, include higher education fairs, thematic university tours, specialized networking sessions, conferences, workshops on academic innovation, and the promotion of doctoral programs. The agency manages a comprehensive online catalogue of over 36,000 study programs, including information on doctoral programs, research units, and partner laboratories, on its multilingual website. More than 50 country-specific websites in 27 languages have been developed. *CampusFrance* also runs a scholarship database with details of nearly 600 scholarship programs for international students. The agency's publications include an annual catalogue of programs taught in English, a general guide to studying and living in France, and studies, analyses, and newsletters designed to raise awareness of mobility and internationalization issues.

In early 2011 a new, expanded *CampusFrance* will be created, to bring together *CampusFrance*, *Égide* and (by the end of 2011) the international section of CNOUS.

This new structure, under the joint supervision of the Ministries of Foreign and European Affairs and Higher Education and Research, will have the status of a public institution and will be responsible for the promotion of French higher education, hosting services for foreign students and researchers, the management of scholarship programs, and the promotion and development of higher education delivered via new technologies.

Since 2006, a system of research and higher education clusters (PRES—*Pôles de Recherche et d'Enseignement Supérieur*) encourages higher education institutions in a region or city to share resources that enhance international visibility and reputation. The member institutions of the PRES collaborate on activities linked to doctoral studies, research, exchange with the private sector and international relations, and increasingly are developing activities in the field of international student services. *Opération Campus*, another government-supported initiative, aims to improve services offered to international students, largely by renovating university facilities with the help of state investment.

Germany

According to OECD (2010), in 2008 Germany hosted 245,522 foreign tertiary students enrolled on courses of a year or more (10.9 percent of total tertiary enrolment) and was the world's third most popular destination, just ahead of France. However, because Germany, like France, counts foreign rather than international students, its totals include long-term residents who are not citizens; incomers can take some time to achieve German citizenship. Between 2000 and 2008 Germany increased its numbers but lost world market share, going down from 9.5 percent to 7.3 percent, while France gained 0.3 percent to reach the same share as Germany (OECD, 2010).

According to figures from *Project Atlas*, Germany hosted 244,776 foreign students in higher education institutions in 2010, compared to 239,143 in 2009 and 233,606 in 2008. These figures, reported by the German Academic Exchange Service (DAAD) (2011), are lower than OECD's figures mainly because DAAD excludes students participating in certain lower tertiary courses that are counted by OECD. Figure 5.10 shows the top 10 sending countries for 2010's foreign students in higher education, though more than half came from countries outside the top 10 (DAAD, 2011).

DAAD's own figures for 2009 showed that, of the 239,143 foreign students enrolled in higher education in that year, 58,921—nearly 25 percent—were *Bildungsinländer*, i.e. had taken their *Abitur* or equivalent exam qualifying them for university entry at a school or college in Germany, or at a German school elsewhere (such as the German school in Moscow) (*Wissenschaft Weltoffen*, 2010). The large majority of "foreign" students in this category are likely to be non-citizen German residents. 180,222 were *Bildungsauslaender*, i.e. had qualified for university entry in a non-German school: only these can be said with confidence to be international students.

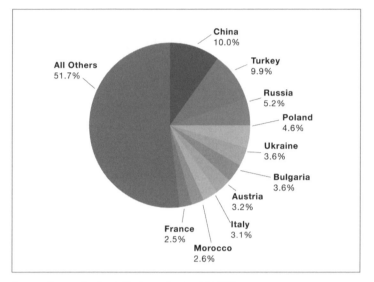

Source: German Academic Exchange Service (DAAD)

In 2008, OECD (2010) records that 94,408 German students traveled to other countries for tertiary studies, 92,391 within the OECD and 2,017 to non-OECD countries. The top 10 countries they went to were Austria (17,464), the Netherlands (16,554), the UK (13,625), Switzerland (10,960), the U.S. (8,917), France (6,918), Australia (1,934), Spain (1,830), New Zealand (1,653), and Hungary (1,640).

Germany's internationalization policies

The German government aims to promote student mobility, both inward and outward, within its broader strategy for the internationalization of science and research. Adopted in February 2008, this strategy outlines four main goals, designed to address the challenges that global competition poses to Germany's science and innovation system. Two of these goals—to strengthen research collaboration with global leaders and to increase long-term cooperation with developing countries in education, research, and development—have direct implications for Germany's mobility efforts. The strategy also outlines policy measures to achieve these goals, including coordinating and bolstering Germany's research presence abroad, analysing international trends in research and innovation and promoting Germany as a hub for research and development in key target countries. The bodies responsible for the implementation of these policies are the German Academic Exchange Service (DAAD), the German Research Foundation (DFG), the Alexander von Humboldt-Foundation (AvH) and—last, but not least—the universities themselves.

The DAAD's programs aim to:

- support students and academics from abroad in order to create lifelong friends of Germany among other countries' future leaders in education, science and research, culture, industry and commerce, politics, and the media;
- support German students and academics abroad, as potential future leaders with international and intercultural experience; and
- build capacity in other countries in support of their economic and democratic reform processes.

The DAAD, largely funded by various federal Ministries, cooperates with the German government in developing new scholarship programs in order to reach student mobility goals and targets; and with foreign governments when negotiating agreements on co-financed scholarship and exchange programs. There are around 250 funding programs for international and German applicants and institutions. Scholarship programs are available for undergraduate, graduate, and doctoral programs, study visits, specialist courses, internships, research placement stays, lectureships, project works, university partnership programs, degree programs, and creating efficient university structures. The most popular and well-established programs for international students are the Study Scholarships for Graduates of All Disciplines; Research Grants for Doctoral Candidates and Young Academics and Scientists; Research Stays for University Academics and Scientists; and the Berlin Artists-in-Residence Program. An increasing number of programs aim to internationalize institutions, for example through dual degree arrangements or improving mentoring for international students. Recently the DAAD set up a new mobility program that offers universities the possibility of applying for funding for scholarships for their own students. The aim is to give more students the opportunity to study abroad and to allow the institution to decide what form the study opportunity will take (internship, semester stay, short-term doctoral stay, etc).

Germany has also improved its immigration laws and policies to support its appeal as an international study destination. For example, the option of remaining in Germany after graduation in order to find employment has been extended; non-EU graduates of German universities can now stay on for up to one year to seek and find a job. A draft law that would have led to stricter visa regulations for individuals or institutions wishing to host international students and scholars was abandoned before entering parliament, in response to representations from the DAAD and others.

Netherlands

According to OECD (2010), in 2008 the Netherlands hosted 40,795 foreign tertiary students enrolled on courses of a year or more (6.8 percent of total tertiary enrollment) and ranked 17th in the list of leading destination countries with 1.2 percent of the world market, up from 0.7 percent in 2000. Nearly three-quarters of the foreign students were international (i.e. non-resident) students.

NUFFIC (the Netherlands Organization for International Cooperation in Higher Education, 2011) reports that the Netherlands hosted over 55,500 foreign/international students in higher education in 2009; this total includes some short-term exchanges and is not comparable with OECD's total for the previous year. Figure 5.11 shows the top 10 sending countries for these 55,500 students; seven of the top senders are other EU countries. Germany alone sends more than 35 percent (NUFFIC, 2011).

FIGURE 5.11: PLACES OF ORIGIN OF INTERNATIONAL STUDENTS IN THE NETHERLANDS, 2009

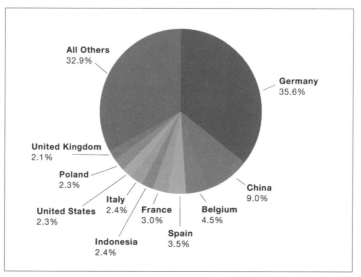

Source: Netherlands Organization for International Cooperation in Higher Education (NUFFIC)

In 2008, OECD records that 13,873 students from the Netherlands travelled to other countries for tertiary studies, just 203 of them to non-OECD countries. The top 10 countries they went to were Belgium (4,056), the UK (3,024), the U.S. (1,682), Germany (1,544), France (652), New Zealand (399), Switzerland (363), Spain (291), Australia, and Sweden (both 249) (OECD, 2010).

The Netherlands' internationalization policies

The Netherlands Ministry of Education, setting out its Internationalization Agenda in 2008, noted that incoming international students help to improve overall quality and performance in Dutch higher education and so benefit domestic students. The Dutch knowledge economy depends on its higher education institutions to attract students from within and outside Europe. After graduation, some of these students can contribute their skills, knowledge, and creativity to the Netherlands labor market. Those who return home or work internationally can be ambassadors for Dutch higher education and build economic, political, and cultural ties between other countries and the Netherlands. For similar reasons, the government thinks it important to send more Dutch students abroad, to benefit from and bring back greater international and intercultural knowledge and skills.

A number of important steps have been taken over the past two decades to facilitate mobility. More English-taught programs have been developed and are being actively marketed, including to students from English-speaking countries faced with high domestic fees. Foreign students who would like to take paid work alongside their studies are allowed to do so (though, depending on nationality, non-EU students can work only for a limited number of hours per week and only if the employer has applied for a work permit). Immigration has become more flexible for international students and so-called "knowledge workers" with the adoption of the new immigration policy and regulations in 2010. However, some obstacles to inward and outward mobility remain. For example, recent national security regulations have made it more difficult for students from certain countries (such as Iran or North Korea) to study in the Netherlands, particularly on programs related to nuclear technology. And Dutch researchers who go abroad on a grant or scholarship may lose out on social security and pension rights.

NUFFIC is responsible for the promotion and marketing of Dutch higher education abroad. Its "Study in Holland" activities aim to attract students to the Netherlands. NUFFIC has established the Holland Alumni Network for foreign students who have previously studied in the country, and supports Dutch students who wish to study abroad by giving them information on the practical, financial, and legal issues. Overseas promotion and marketing are focused on specific places of origin through a network of ten Netherlands Education Support Offices (NESOs), located in China, India, Indonesia, Brazil, Vietnam, Thailand, Mexico, Russia, Taiwan, and South Korea. NESOs promote Dutch higher education in their countries, support Dutch institutions active in or cooperating with them, advise local students on learning opportunities in the Netherlands, collect and disseminate information on local education, and support local alumni networks.

NUFFIC also administers a range of international scholarship programs for outbound and inbound students (e.g. the Huygens Scholarship Program and Netherlands Fellowships Programs); raises awareness of the importance of international cooperation with policy makers and other relevant stakeholders; conducts mobility research; aims continuously to improve national and international mobility data; and publishes an annual *Internationalisation Monitor*. The Netherlands Ministry of Foreign Affairs finances a number of education capacity-building programs for developing countries, which NUFFIC manages: for example, the NICHE program that aims to strengthen post-secondary education and training institutions in 23 developing countries.

Services to Dutch tertiary institutions include checking and certifying the degrees and prior qualifications offered by applicants (NUFFIC also serves as the National Academic Recognition Information Centre, or NARIC, for the Netherlands); supporting them in international student recruitment; brokering international partnership and collaboration arrangements; and providing consultancy services. As of 2009, NUFFIC offers a self-evaluation and benchmarking tool, called MINT (Mapping Internationalization), with which universities can map and compare their internationalization efforts.

Spain

OECD (2010) reports that in 2008 Spain hosted 64,906 foreign tertiary students on courses of a year or more (3.6 percent of total tertiary enrollment, 5.3 percent of those enrolled on Type B tertiary programs and 24 percent of those enrolled on advanced research programs). These numbers put Spain 10th in the world list of destination countries, with 1.9 percent of the world market, up from 1.3 percent in 2000. Nearly 6 in 10 of the foreign students were international (i.e. non-resident) students (OECD, 2010).

According to figures from *Project Atlas* (2011), Spain hosted 65,568 foreign students in 2009, but again these figures may not be comparable with OECD's for the previous year. Figure 5.12 shows the top 10 sending countries for these students (*Fundación Universidad.es*, 2011).

FIGURE 5.12: PLACES OF ORIGIN OF FOREIGN STUDENTS IN SPAIN, 2008/9

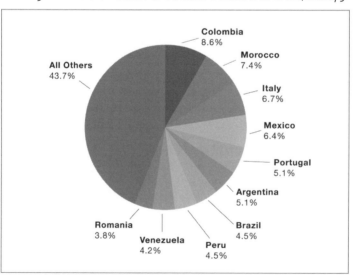

Source: Ministry of Education of Spain.
Note: The data in the figure refers to "foreign students" only and not to "mobile students."

According to OECD, in 2008 24,983 Spanish students were enrolled on tertiary courses overseas lasting at least a year, of whom just 326 went to non-OECD countries. The top 10 destinations for Spanish students were the UK (5,739), Germany (4,692), France (3,905), the U.S. (3,664), Switzerland (1,520), Belgium (886), the Netherlands (812), Portugal (613), Italy (504), and Austria (473) (OECD, 2010).

Spain's internationalization policies

In October 2008, the Spanish government, alongside regional governments and Spanish universities, approved the creation of a foundation for the international promotion of Spanish universities— *Fundación Universidad.es*. The main purpose was to create an international brand for the Spanish university system and to improve the international visibility of Spanish universities, both public and private. One of this agency's main tasks is to promote student mobility in Spain, establishing the country as a leading destination for international students and researchers and increasing the presence of Spanish students and researchers throughout the world. The country aims to attract international students in line with the growing priority placed on internationalization among Spanish institutions, which includes creating an international and multicultural environment on university campuses and contributing to capacity building in developing countries through the establishment of mobility programs.

Fundación Universidad.es works closely with all government departments with national and regional responsibilities for higher education, including the Ministry of Education, the Ministry of Foreign Affairs and Cooperation and the Spanish Agency for International Development and Cooperation. To address some of the present hindrances to mobility and exchange—particularly the bureaucratic processes involved in obtaining a visa to study or conduct research in Spain—the agency is setting up a working group of stakeholders to propose solutions.

Fundación Universidad.es represents both public and private higher education institutions and works closely with them, individually and through the Conference of Rectors of Spanish Universities. The agency is developing strategies to attract students and researchers from countries considered strategically important in Spain's international higher education market, including Argentina, Brazil, Chile, China, Colombia, Equatorial Guinea, India, Italy, Morocco, Mexico, Portugal, Russia, the Syrian Arab Republic, Saudi Arabia, and the United States. An international website has been set up, on which interested international students and researchers can find comprehensive information on Spanish universities and their academic programs, a complete and updated scholarships database, and information on the formal and legal requirements for organizing an academic stay in Spain. Additionally, an online student and researcher service has been launched, allowing users to contact *Fundación Universidad.es* by phone, by e-mail, or live through the new Chat system.

Fundación Universidad.es has also worked with sister organizations abroad to organize higher education fairs focused on graduate courses in different countries of

Latin America, and has participated in a similar European initiative in the Asia region. While the agency does not currently collect primary data on student mobility, it works with the Ministry of Education to improve the quality of the international higher education data they collect in an effort to conform to international standards. A project to collect data on mobility of students, researchers, lecturers, and university staff, gathered directly from Spanish universities, has been launched and results should start to come through in 2011. The agency's current information on student mobility in Spain shows that further efforts are needed to increase the country's attractions to international students.

Sweden

OECD (2010) reports that in 2008 Sweden hosted 34,556 foreign tertiary students on courses of a year or more (8.5 percent of total tertiary enrollment, 23.7 percent of those enrolled on advanced research programs), putting Sweden 19th in the world list of destination countries, with 1 percent of the world market, down from 1.3 percent in 2000, though numbers have increased by 35 percent over that period. Around 2 in 3 of the foreign students were international (i.e. non-resident) students (OECD, 2010).

According to figures from *Project Atlas* (2011), Sweden had 36,600 foreign/international students enrolled in 2009. Figure 5.13 shows the top 10 sending countries for these students. Sweden is another country where more than half the international students come from places outside of the top 10 (Swedish Institute, 2011).

In 2008, according to OECD, 15,455 Swedish students were enrolled on tertiary courses overseas lasting at least a year, of whom 513 went to non-OECD countries. Their top 10 destinations were the U.S. (3,296), the UK (3,194), Denmark (1,796), Norway (1,290), Austria (853), Poland (725), Germany (612), Finland (532), France (441), and Hungary (331) (OECD, 2010).

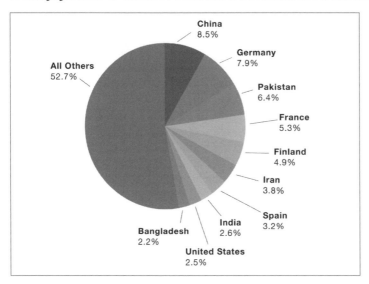

Source: Swedish Institute

Sweden's internationalization policies

Successive Swedish governments have regarded internationalization of higher education as important. Inward mobility is valued for internationalizing the study experience of Swedish students who do not go abroad and for improving the quality of Swedish higher education. Development aid has also been an important motive, although there has been concern in recent years that too much focus on inbound mobility could lead to brain drain from some lower income countries. Public diplomacy has not been a very prominent motive for attracting international students in the past, although there are signs that it might be given more weight in the future. Other motives that are likely to become more important are skills shortages in Sweden, and the connection between attracting foreign students and attracting foreign investments.

Until now, international students in Sweden have been funded in the same way as national students (i.e. through government funding to higher education institutions), and have rarely been required to pay any kind of tuition fees. However, in the last decade, a sharp increase in the number of English-taught courses, a consequential increase in the number of inbound students and the rise of the global education market have led the government to review and change its policy. Beginning in 2011, students from non-EU countries will be charged the full cost of their studies in Sweden. This is partly to offset the mounting costs of international students, partly because the government believes that Sweden should attract foreign students by the quality of its higher education, not by free tuition. However, the government also plans to provide at least 90 Million SEK (about $12 million) for scholarships, partly aimed at students from lower income countries.

The Swedish Institute, a government agency for public and cultural diplomacy, has supported international mobility in higher education since the 1940s by providing scholarships for inbound and outbound students, many of these through bilateral agreements with other countries. Since the 1970s there have been development-aid-funded scholarships for Masters and Ph.D. studies in Sweden. Since the late 1990s, the government has funded extensive scholarship programs aimed at exchange with countries in Eastern Europe and the former Soviet Union. Since 1989, Swedish students have been able to obtain loans to study abroad. Sweden has participated in Erasmus and Erasmus Mundus, the EU-sponsored mobility scheme, since 1992; the number of outbound Erasmus and Erasmus Mundus students is now around 30,000 per year.

The increase already mentioned in the number of English-taught programs at Master's level, along with an increase in the number of international students, led to a balance being achieved between the number of inbound and the number of outbound students in the early 2000s. Since then there have been more inbound than outbound students, which has led the government to try to stimulate outbound mobility by funding teacher mobility and encouraging the study of more foreign languages in secondary schools.

Mobility programs are managed and funded through several government offices and private organizations. The International Programme Office (IPK) handles the administration of EU programs (including Erasmus and Erasmus Mundus) and several aid-funded programs that also promote mobility. STINT, The Foundation for the Internationalization of Research, has also funded inbound mobility. The Swedish Institute cooperates with IPK, STINT, and the Swedish National Agency for Higher Education (HSV) to promote and advocate for student mobility. The Swedish Institute also works with higher education institutions within Sweden; in 2008, the Institute and 29 higher education institutions jointly launched a collaborative project to promote Sweden as a study destination.

The Swedish Institute administers ten scholarship programs for international students and researchers from different regions and countries. Approximately 1,000 international students receive these funding awards for short- and long-term academic visits. International students in Ph.D. programs and researchers receive scholarships for six or twelve months; Masters students can receive funding for up to two years. Though these are the general guidelines, funding duration can vary by program. A scholarship program financed by the Pakistan Higher Education Commission enables Pakistani students to spend up to six years in Sweden to gain both a master's degree and a Ph.D. Under the Baltic Sea Region Exchange program to support cooperation in education and research between Sweden and Belarus, Estonia, Latvia, Lithuania, Poland, Russia, and Ukraine, funding is available to students, teachers, researchers, administrators, and doctoral students in high school education, adult education, undergraduate studies, and advanced research, for projects or networking activities, individual scholarships, or short-term visit grants.

While the Swedish Institute does not collect mobility data—this is done by the Swedish National Agency for Higher Education (HSV) and Statistics Sweden—the Institute undertakes research on international student experiences and perceptions. Findings from this research have been used to promote Sweden as a study destination and to make the case for policies that will attract more international students to Sweden in the future.

OCEANIA

Australia

According to OECD (2010), Australia ranked fifth in the world in 2008 as a destination for tertiary students, with 230,635 international students (6.9 percent of the world market) enrolled for a year or more, making up 20.6 percent of the country's tertiary enrollment—the highest percentage in the world—and 23.3 percent of enrollment on advanced research programs (OECD, 2010). In 2008 Australia also had over 174,000 international students on VET courses, nearly 126,000 on English language courses and over 31,000 on other courses: in 2009 these figures rose to over 232,000 on VET, over 135,000 on English language courses and over 33,000 on other courses (Australian Education International website, retrieved January 2011).

Figure 5.14 shows which countries were the top 10 senders of tertiary students to Australia in 2009. These figures may include short-term exchanges (Australian Education International [AEI], 2011).

In 2008, 10,206 students from Australia were enrolled in tertiary courses of a year or more in other countries, 9,777 of them in OECD countries and 430 elsewhere. Within the OECD their most popular destinations were the U.S. (3,091), New Zealand (2,852), the UK (1,610), Canada (458), Germany (354), Japan (337), and France (297) (OECD, 2010).

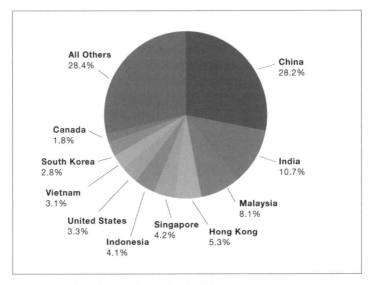

Source: Australian Education International (AEI)

Until recently, Australia has been extremely successful in growing its numbers of international students. Its aggressively-marketed tertiary education system offers a wide range of products to suit all tastes and requirements; it has good universities, including several new, private universities, boasting state-of-the-art facilities closer to home for many Asian students than Europe or America; it has had the reputation of being an immigration-friendly country for students; and, like the U.S., it has benefited greatly from a surge of interest from Chinese students.

However, in the past year there have been concerns within Australia about international student enrollments falling. Total enrollments by international students declined by 1.6 percent in January - November 2010 compared with the same period in 2009, mainly due to steep drops in numbers in English-language classes (down 17.6 percent, new enrollments down 21.3 percent) (Australian Education International website, retrieved January 2011). Higher education institutions are still experiencing a rise in enrollments by students from abroad, but though total enrollments rose 8.5 percent in the year to November, new enrollments rose just 2.4 percent; the institutions predict that numbers will decline in 2012, partly because English-language institutes often feed students into universities. Indian enrollments in Australian university courses have already fallen by 19.3 per cent (new enrollments by 44.8 percent), following attacks on Indian students in 2008 and 2009. Also, the rising value of the Australian dollar has been increasing the costs to international students of higher study in Australia, to U.S. levels or beyond.

The final and potentially biggest cause of falling enrollments has been the changes made to student visa rules by Australian federal and state governments keen to sever the link between education and immigration. As in the UK, there is a tension and some incompatibility between education policies on the one hand and immigration policies on the other. In Australia too there have been investigations into private colleges suspected of offering poor-quality courses to "bogus students" primarily interested in acquiring permanent resident status. International students hoping to study in Australia are now required to show the capacity to pay for three years of living and tuition costs before receiving a student visa, which is estimated to be three times greater than similar requirements in Britain, Canada, New Zealand, and the United States. Significant changes in Australia's student visa approval process have made it harder for students to get visas, and, perhaps more importantly, to obtain permanent residency after graduation from the vocational education and training sector, where students frequently enrolled in short-term certificate programs in order to qualify for permanent residency. In addition, Australia has tightened its criteria for admitting skilled immigrants, among other things raising the requirements for English language skills and previous work experience.

Speakers at the Australian International Education Conference in October 2010 called on the national government and state governments to halt the decline by revising student immigration rules, subsidizing student housing, and making other policy changes (See Kremmer, October 13, 2011; and Kremmer, October 15, 2011). A review of the student visa regime was announced in December. However, the Department of Immigration's Red Book, released on January 4, 2011, notes that the number of international student visa applications being approved has already dropped by almost a third in 2009/10 compared to 2008/9, and is likely to fall further in 2010/11; and that whereas previously a third of international students might have expected to apply for and attain permanent residency, under the latest immigration rules less than a sixth would succeed. The Red Book forecasts that overseas student arrivals will drop more than half from early 2010 levels by June 2014 ("Aussie Education Market," January 11, 2011).

Australia's internationalization policies

International education and mobility has been actively promoted and supported by the Australian government for decades, in order to foster long-lasting education, research, and professional ties between individuals, institutions, and countries.

Australia's policies to support inbound student mobility aim to ensure that Australia is seen as a welcoming and good-value place to study for a globally-recognized qualification; enhance international awareness of Australia as a leader in education, research, and learning; showcase Australia's innovativeness, quality, and global reputation for world-class education, training, and research; and ensure that Australia's education and training industry has the support and assistance it needs for sustainable growth.

Australia was one of the inaugural countries involved in establishing the University Mobility in Asia and the Pacific (UMAP) program in 1993. This program was set up to support partnerships, credit transfer, and institutional relationships that foster student mobility in the Asia Pacific Region. Currently, the Australian UMAP Student Exchange Programme provides funding to Australian higher education institutions to subsidize the cost of establishing and monitoring Australian students' participation in UMAP student exchanges with counterpart higher education institutions in the region. Eligible student exchanges benefit from tuition fee waivers and credit transfer. Australian higher education institutions receive A$5,000 per student to subsidize the cost of the student's participation in an eligible student exchange. The UMAP program has played a part in helping Australia to become a magnet center, attracting international students from the whole Asia Pacific region.

Through Australian Education International (AEI) in the Department of Education, Employment & Workplace Relations, the government sponsors several programs to support inbound student mobility. A$6.5m per annum is provided to universities and VET organizations for scholarships, to enable them to assist incoming and outgoing mobility and to support the establishment of long-term exchange partnerships. A$27m per annum is available for Endeavor Awards to support graduate, VET and professional training, research, and international collaborations. AEI also funds research to provide more accurate statistical data on student mobility, a snapshot of the demographic make-up of students in Australia, and an overview of current student mobility practices at Australian universities.

The Australian government is also committed to supporting Australian students to engage in study abroad. Outbound mobility is seen as a mechanism for improving the quality of education that Australian graduates receive so that Australian business remains internationally competitive; for providing students with intercultural competence, skills and knowledge; and for giving Australian students the opportunity to become global citizens and communicators.

Activities the Australian government has initiated and sponsored to assist outward student mobility include:

- An Overseas Study Portal that consolidates information about overseas study opportunities for Australian students into one easy-to-access site;

- The Forum on Outbound Mobility Roundtables, a series of industry-led discussions held to examine the major issues affecting the mobility of Australian students;

- The Vocational Education Outbound Mobility Programme, which funds projects to increase the number of Australian VET students undertaking an international study experience and to increase the level of partnerships between Australian and international VET training providers and industry.

- The EU/Australia Cooperation in Higher Education and VET projects, which aim to develop joint credit transfer arrangements, support academic cooperation, and encourage student mobility between Australia and the EU.

New Zealand

New Zealand ranked twelfth in the world in 2008 as a tertiary destination, according to OECD, with 59,636 foreign students enrolled for a year or more, making up 1.8 percent of the world market—a big increase since 2000 when the country had a market share of just 0.4 percent. International students made up 12.9 percent of New Zealand's tertiary enrollment and 31.3 percent of its enrollment on advanced research programs; foreign students made up 24.4 percent of tertiary enrollment and 46.9 percent of enrollment in advanced research programs (OECD, 2010).

The New Zealand Ministry of Education (2011) reports that there were 95,500 international fee-paying students in New Zealand in 2009. Figure 5.15 shows which countries sent the most tertiary students to New Zealand in that year (New Zealand Ministry of Education, 2011). The total projected in *Project Atlas* for 2009 is much larger than the OECD total for 2008 just quoted, because they were collected on a different basis; however, the New Zealand Ministry of Education has reported that international student numbers grew by 6 percent between 2008 and 2009, and by a further 5 percent in the first eight months of 2010 compared to the same period in 2009 ("A third of foreign students stay on, minister says." February 17, 2011). According to OECD, in 2008 the top 10 sending countries of students enrolled for at least a year were China, India, UK, U.S., Australia, Malaysia, South Korea, Germany, South Africa, and Fiji, in that order.

In 2008, 4,863 students from New Zealand were enrolled in tertiary courses of a year or more in other countries, 4,152 of them in OECD countries and 111 elsewhere. Within the OECD their most popular destinations were Australia (2,085), the U.S. (1,022), the UK (508), and Canada (145) (OECD, 2010).

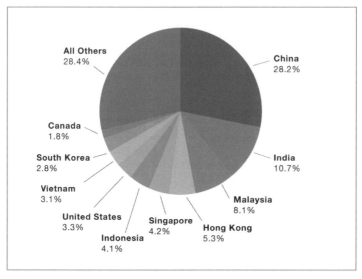

Source: New Zealand Ministry of Education
Note: These data include "fee-paying" students for calendar year 2009.

New Zealand's internationalization policies

The New Zealand government encourages international students to enroll with public and private education providers. The benefits are seen as increasing recognition of New Zealand qualifications, providing fee revenues for providers (in the 2007/8 financial year, international students benefited the economy by NZ$2.1 billion), and expanding the international awareness of NZ students. The New Zealand government's policies to support international student mobility began with the Education Act 1989, legislation that explicitly authorized the recruitment of international fee-paying students by public education providers (including schools, universities, and technical institutes). Following marked growth in international student enrollments, a compulsory "Code of Practice for the Pastoral Care of International Students" was introduced by the Ministry of Education in 2002, and amended in 2003 and 2010. The Code of Practice must be followed by any education provider that enrolls international students.

Since 2004, the government has funded the international promotion of New Zealand education as a national brand and has offered scholarships for top doctoral and undergraduate students. These and other programs are administered by the lead sector body for international education, the Education New Zealand Trust. The funding of national promotion efforts is also supported through the compulsory Export Education Levy, which has been charged to education providers since 2003.

The rate of the Export Education Levy is 0.45 percent of tuition revenues from international students.

In order to attract more research students to New Zealand universities, the government has since 2006 allowed international students pursuing Ph.D. programs to pay domestic student fee rates instead of international student rates, which are normally higher. As a result, total enrollments of international Ph.D. students in New Zealand's eight universities rose from 693 during 2005 to 2,405 during 2009. The Ministry of Education funds a small number of Doctoral Research Scholarships for selected international students.

The Ministry also validates the requirements for student exchange programs run by education providers (schools and universities) and employs a network of education counselors working in New Zealand embassies in particular countries, notably in China, India, Saudi Arabia, the European Union, Malaysia, and Chile. The counselors are responsible for building inter-agency relationships with the education authorities in the country where they are based, and help to promote New Zealand's education system and qualifications structure.

The Ministry of Education collects data on enrollments of international students by course, institution type, and nationality, and on the fee revenues earned by education providers. These data, used to form the basis of economic assessments of the value of international education to New Zealand, have encouraged the government and the tertiary education sector to increase their promotional activities so as to attract more international students. In contrast to attitudes in Australia, New Zealand's Immigration Minister was pleased to announce recently that about a third of the international students who come to New Zealand to study stay on afterwards and around one fifth become permanent residents. "Not only does New Zealand gain from the economic benefits of having them study here, many international students stay on, providing longer-term benefits by contributing their skills to our workforce and economy," he said ("A third of foreign students stay on, minister says" February 17, 2011).

AFRICA

South Africa

African countries contribute around 10 percent of the world total of international students. Close to 6 percent of all students from the region study overseas, three times more than the global average. In some countries, 30 percent or more of tertiary students study abroad. South Africa, Nigeria, and Ethiopia have the lowest outbound ratios, ranging from 0.8 percent to 2 percent.

Within Africa, South Africa is the leading host destination. South Africa reported 63,9640 international students in South Africa's 23 public universities in 2010, representing 8 percent of the total student population (see the *Atlas of Student Mobility* website: www.iie.org/projectatlas). This figure understates the true scale of inward mobility as it does not include students at private institutions, which cannot be officially recognized as universities. In 2008, according to OECD, South Africa was the 11th most popular destination country in the world—see Chart 2.1 in Chapter 2— and among the top 20 host nations for American students. In 2007 it enrolled around 2 percent of the world's globally mobile tertiary students, and just 0.8 percent of its own tertiary students studied in other countries. Most of South Africa's international students come from within Africa, primarily from neighboring and turbulent Zimbabwe. Figure 5.16 shows the top 10 places of origin for international students in South Africa (International Education Association of South Africa, 2011).

OECD (2010) reports that in 2008 7,572 South Africans were enrolled on courses lasting at least a year in other countries' tertiary systems, 6,798 of them in OECD countries. Their most popular OECD destinations were the U.S. (1,622), the UK (1,539), New Zealand (1,409), Australia (768), and Canada (499) (OECD, 2010).

FIGURE 5.16: PLACES OF ORIGIN FOR INTERNATIONAL STUDENTS IN SOUTH AFRICA, 2008

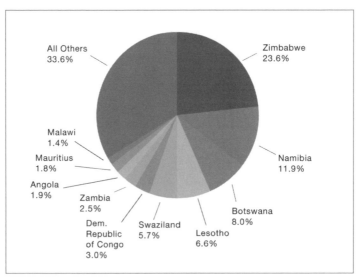

Source: International Education Association of South Africa (IEASA)

South Africa's internationalization policies

South Africa's Department of Home Affairs has embarked on an improvement scheme to facilitate inbound student mobility, including reviewing the presently onerous application processes for study visas and visitors permits for researchers and scholars. The Department is also developing a closer working relationship with the International Education Association of South Africa (IEASA), a nonprofit organization established to help universities and universities of technology in South Africa to respond to international educational trends, which has been promoting internationalization since its inception in 1997.

IEASA establishes international contacts for relationship building that will benefit students and tertiary institutions and will assist South Africa to compete in world markets. IEASA's annual publication, "Study South Africa," which includes a profile of each South African (public) university and is available on the Internet, is an important international marketing tool. IEASA also monitors government policy and procedures on issues affecting international students and academic visitors from abroad, and represents their interests to the government and within South Africa.

South Africa also hopes that the country's raised international profile since successfully hosting the World Cup soccer games in 2010 will also generate more interest in coming to South Africa for higher education.

Conclusions on the Impact of National Policies

Chapter 4 reviewed the factors that push students toward study abroad; that deter others who might have wished to study abroad; and that pull internationally mobile students toward particular countries or institutions. Countries that wish to attract international students and persuade their own to study abroad need to align their national policies with the motivations of potentially mobile students.

This is of course easier to say than to do. Some features—such as whether or not a country is geographically convenient for other countries with growing demand for education and inadequate domestic provision—cannot be changed. Others—such as the size, quality, and relevance of a national higher education system—can be changed if the national political will, determination, and resources are there, but change will take a long time. Most other aspects can be addressed through national policies. The policies of the countries highlighted in this chapter show many successes, and a few cautionary tales.

Helpful policies

If the aim is to boost inbound mobility, it is clearly helpful to **ensure that students can find in your country something they cannot get—or not in the right quantity, quality, or at the right level—at home.** The traditional leading destination countries have large, high quality, diverse education systems already, and their challenge is to keep them that way. Others must build them up (Australia has, China is, India is trying to) or develop "niche markets" in an area of strength—such as VET, Type B tertiary provision, graduate or advanced research programs, or particular subject fields. English-language tuition is a niche market; it need not be confined to Anglophone countries, as Sweden, the Netherlands and others demonstrate.

It is not enough for a country to have attractive provision available. Potential **students must be made aware of it, be convinced that it is more attractive than their alternatives, and be given all the practical information and help they require to access it.** The countries that manage this best are those that make generous amounts of government money available for marketing; market effectively, assuring mobile students of a warm welcome in their country, in student-friendly ways and on the home turf of target students; market their institutions collectively rather than allowing them to compete against each other or leaving some out (such as private or non-university institutions); and have well-resourced national organizations able to act as "one-stop shops" for the information and practical help international students may seek, before and during study. A single national organization handling all international student business, like Japan's JASSO or NUFFIC in the Netherlands, is probably the ideal arrangement.

Financial considerations are very important to all students except those from the most affluent families in each country. National policies that **keep international students' tuition fees and maintenance costs modest, or offset them** with widely-known and widely-available scholarship or other support, can tip the scales of student decisions. The example of France shows how much countries can grow their inbound numbers and strengthen their market share if the government is content to subsidize a large part of international students' costs. The example of Sweden shows that even the most internationally-minded governments may find this policy unsustainable in the long-term. Now that internationally mobile students are increasingly favoring newer, regional, better-value destinations over the traditional, expensive destination countries that charge international students full costs (the U.S., the UK, now also Australia), traditional destinations wishing to maintain their numbers will need either to increase cost offsets or to boost their non-financial attractions dramatically.

Attractive, affordable study opportunities are not enough if international students cannot get into the country to take them up, so governments need to **ensure that immigration and visa rules are student-friendly.** The case of international students needs to be considered before, rather than after, general immigration principles are established; this often requires co-operation between different government departments not in the habit of co-operating. It is also helpful if immigration rules permit work during study to help defray course costs. A single, national organization working with education institutions to represent international students' interests within a country can often be a powerful advocate for student-friendly immigration policies (as was DAAD in Germany, see above).

It is helpful also if national policies to increase mobility at or within the tertiary level **take account of the fact that education is a ladder.** If internationally mobile students can get onto a lower rung of the ladder they are more likely to progress to a higher rung within the same country. The U.S. operates excellent exchange visitor arrangements covering a wide range of educational opportunities. As shown in Chapter 3 and in Part II, there is significant evidence that young people who come to the U.S. during secondary education, for a non-degree course or on other types of short-term exchange visit, often go on to degree courses at U.S. universities or colleges. Similarly, undergraduate courses lead to graduate courses, and graduate courses to research, academic or teaching posts, within the U.S. As mentioned above, Australian higher education institutions have been very concerned with recent falls in enrollments on English courses, because they know that when those enrollments fall, university enrollments will fall soon afterwards. Astute national policy-makers open up their education system to international students at all levels, from secondary school onwards, for both academic and vocational courses.

It is also useful for national policies to **ensure that international students in the country are well-looked-after.** New Zealand's introduction of a mandatory "Code of Practice for the Pastoral Care of International Students" has paid dividends, whereas Australia has seen a big drop in Indian enrollments following some local hostility towards Indian students. Many countries now host large numbers of Chinese students, and as Chapter 4 noted, safety is a major concern for Chinese families. Countries that charge international students high fees run a particular risk that they will feel alienated if not given good pastoral care and full value for their money.

Maintaining links with past international students through **alumni networks** will also help them to remember their host country fondly, recommend it to compatriots, and keep up international friendships through later careers, benefitting both countries.

Helpful policies **to promote outbound mobility,** long-term or short-term, include **providing practical information and assistance; supporting outgoing students financially** (with grants and scholarships or by giving them the same student support they would get at home); **and government support for international collaborative education ventures.**

Unhelpful policies

Unhelpful policies—many of them the obverse of the helpful policies just mentioned—include:

- **Overcharging international students,** i.e. allowing prices to rise to a level above the value of the courses provided, or which discourage all but the most affluent. This can happen when international students are valued primarily for their contribution to straitened national and institutional finances.

- Failing to provide comprehensive care and support for international students. All countries have good intentions, but fragmented responsibilities, insufficient government backing or resources, turf wars between Ministries, lack of urgency in addressing problems, and poorly-managed education institutions can all damage care and support. Then international students return home not as ambassadors for the host country but to warn others against studying there.

- Immigration and visa policies that fail to recognize, or are not adapted for, international students' special circumstances. The new UK government is having difficulties with pre-election promises to limit non-EU immigration, which included international students and scholars as if they were all potential long-term immigrant workers. U.S. arrangements, by contrast, distinguish clearly and enforceably between immigrant visas and the non-immigrant visas given to students, exchange visitors, most scholars, and many academics and teachers.

- Immigration and visa policies that discriminate unreasonably against some groups of international students. Discrimination against a group can be reasonable, for example keeping students of certain nationalities away from nuclear technology courses on national security grounds. It is far less reasonable to make entry more difficult for students wishing to enter private as opposed to public institutions, or non-degree or VET courses as opposed to degree courses. There are other, better ways of keeping out "bogus students"; quality education at any level is valuable; all levels are part of the education ladder; and tertiary enrollments will suffer as a result.

---

[1] This project is under review and is contingent upon continued funding. On November 19, 2010, the *Chronicle of Higher Education* reported that the Global 30 Program may be eliminated. According to the article, government cuts have "shaved up to 30 percent from the budget allocated to each institution," and the "government's Budget Review Committee, which is trying to slash...the country's runaway public debt," has voted to restructure the project.

UNITED STATES

Introduction

This country study focuses on inward educational mobility to the United States. Individuals coming to the U.S. for educational purposes are uniquely well documented, not least because everyone who wishes to come to the U.S. as an international student, and who does not have a U.S. passport or permanent resident card, needs a nonimmigrant visa. We can therefore gain a complete picture of inward student mobility from visa information.

- Section A outlines the U.S. visa system and looks at overall numbers of students coming to the U.S. for education-related purposes.

- Section B considers inward mobility for college and university education, drawing on the extensive databases of the Institute of International Education (IIE) and published visa information.

- Section C considers inward mobility for all education-related purposes under Exchange Visitor arrangements. The authors are extremely grateful to the U.S. Department of State for sharing with us unpublished Exchange Visitor (J-1 visa) statistics for the years 2006–09.

Section A

U.S. visa arrangements and overall numbers

International students may arrive in the U.S. under F-1, J-1, or M-1 visas.

- **F-1 visas** are for foreign students undertaking academic programs at American language schools, public high schools, private schools, universities, and other higher education institutions. The school or institution needs to have been approved by the U.S. Citizenship and Immigration Service (USCIS) to accept foreign students. Study must be full time, but F-1 visa students may, while enrolled, work on their institution's campus or gain practical work experience in their field of study. They may also take practical training as a full-time employee after completing degree courses. To gain an F-1 visa, potential students must show that they intend to return to their country of residence and can maintain themselves financially throughout their stay. F-1 visas are granted for a set period related to the expected length of study, though they are limited to 12 months for attendance at U.S. public high schools.

- **J-1 visas** are for those classified as Exchange Visitors. There are a number of J-1 visa categories, with different minimum and maximum lengths and conditions attached, covering a wide range of visitors, the great majority of them coming to America wholly or partly for educational purposes. We will describe these categories more fully in section C.

- **M-1 visas** are for foreign students undertaking vocational training provided by institutions approved for the purpose by USCIS. Institutions approved to take M-1 students are often flight schools (including the five institutions with the highest number of students holding M-1 visas) or trade schools.

To establish the full numbers coming to the U.S. for educational purposes, it may be necessary to look at statistics for more than one of the above types of visa. Secondary school, college, and university students may come to the U.S. under either F-1 visas, if they are self-funded and making their own arrangements, or J-1 visas, if they meet the conditions of the relevant Exchange Visitor scheme. Similarly, vocational training can be undertaken on either a J-1 visa or an M-1 visa, depending on the field of study, the institution attended, and whether sponsored scheme conditions are met. However, the J-1 visa is the only nonimmigrant visa option for many education-related categories of visitors, including Au Pairs, Camp Counselors, Summer Work/Travelers, Professors, Teachers, Research Scholars, and Short-term Scholars.

Overall numbers can be analyzed either on the basis of individuals currently active (enrolled) in educational programs, or on the basis of individuals starting or ending their program participation in a particular time period.

The Management Summary reports from the U.S. Department of Homeland Security's Student and Exchange Visitor Program (SEVP) give snapshot information on "currently active" F-1, M-1, and J-1 visa holders at the end of each quarter. The latest report available at the time of writing states that **on June 30, 2010, there were 957,748 individuals actively undertaking F-1, M-1, or J-1 visa programs, of which 733,430 were F-1 or M-1 visa-holders, and 224,318 were J-1 visa-holders.** The difference between numbers under F-1/M-1 and J-1 arrangements is likely to be less marked, however, when we consider individuals starting or ending their programs in a particular year. F-1 visitors typically enroll on longer programs than J-1 visitors, meaning that the number of J-1 visitors over the course of any particular year is higher.

Chart II.1 below is based on SEVP figures, and shows the education level or category of the 733,430 Student Visitors (i.e., F-1 and M-1 visa holders) who were "active" in June 2010. As chart II.1 shows, 6,998 of these Student Visitors, or just less than 1 percent, were on flight training or other vocational training, so they would have held M-1 visas. Of the 726,432 holding F-1 visas, 40.9 percent were graduate students, 29.3 percent undergraduate students, 3.4 percent secondary students, 1.8 percent primary students, and just 176 (0.02 percent) were high school students. It seems likely that most of the school students holding F-1 visas were in the U.S. as a result of their parents' movements and decisions rather than their own educational aspirations, particularly at primary school level. At secondary and high school levels, given the United States's tradition of encouraging "high school years abroad," more international students will have decided on the move themselves, to broaden their personal experience and/or help them get into a U.S. university or college—but if so, they may well be in the U.S. on J-1 visas. (The distribution of Exchange Visitors [i.e., J-1 visa holders] between education levels and categories will be given in section C.)

CHART II.1: STUDENT VISITORS TO U.S. BY LEVEL (JUNE 2010)

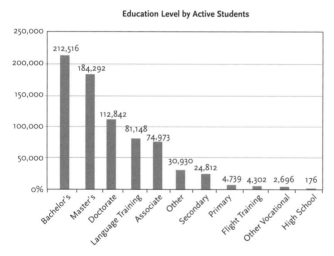

Education Level by Active Students

Source: Student and Exchange Visitor System, General Summary Quarterly Review for the quarter ending June 30, 2010. http://www.aila.org/content/default.aspx?docid=32693

Section B

<u>College and university students</u>

IIE's 2010 *Open Doors* report tells us that in 2009/10, 690,923 international students (defined as those who are not citizens, permanent residents, or refugees) were enrolled in U.S. higher education institutions, making up 3.5 percent of total U.S. higher education enrollment. International student numbers have risen every year for the past four years, but the 2009/10 increase of 2.9 percent over 2008/9 was the lowest. In 2005/6 there were 564,766 international students; in 2006/7 there were 582,984 (an increase of 3.2 percent); in 2007/08 there were 623,805 (an increase of 7 percent); and in 2008/9 there were 671,616 (an increase of 7.7 percent).

Open Doors 2009 indicates that only a small minority of college and university students are Exchange Visitors. In 2008/9, 6 percent of international tertiary students were on J-1 visas (down from a peak of 13 percent in 1989/90, when overall numbers were much smaller), 88 percent on F-1 visas and 6 percent on M-1 or other visas. Most *Open Doors* figures do not distinguish between the different visa categories, so the information in the following paragraphs relates to *all* international students at U.S. universities and colleges, including the J-1 visa-holders who will be analyzed separately in section C.

Of the 690,923 international students enrolled in U.S. colleges and universities in 2009/10, 623,119 were on academic programs and 67,804 (9.8 percent) were undertaking Optional Practical Training. Of those on academic programs, 68,562 (11.0 percent) were studying at associate's level; 205,869 (33.0 percent) at the bachelor's level; 293,885 (47.2 percent) at the graduate level, including 116,254 (18.7 percent) at the doctoral level; and 54,803 (8.8 percent) on non-degree courses. Compared to the international students enrolled in 2008/9, numbers studying at associate level had fallen by 7.4 percent, but numbers in all other categories had increased—by 5.8 percent for non-degree students, 5.1 percent for undergraduate students, 3.7 percent for graduate students, and 1.8 percent for those on Optional Practical Training.

As table II.1 shows, new college and university enrollments by international students rose by 1.3 percent in 2009/10, much less than in the previous three years, and would have fallen if not for strong growth in non-degree enrollments. New graduate and undergraduate enrollments fell.

LEVEL	2006/7	%	2007/8	%	2008/9	%	2009/10 (% CHANGE)	
UNDERGRADUATE	63,749	40.6	68,195	39.4	82,136	41.0	79,365 (-3.4%)	39.1
POSTGRADUATE	72,726	46.3	78,489	45.3	84,828	42.3	84,613 (-0.3%)	41.7
NON-DEGREE	20,703	13.2	26,437	15.3	33,496	16.7	38,992 (+16.4%)	19.2
TOTAL	157,178		173,121		200,460		202,970	
% CHANGE	+ 10%		+ 10.1%		+ 15.8%		+1.3%	

Source: Chow, P. and Bhandari, R. (2010). Open doors 2010: Report on international educational exchange. New York: Institute for International Education.

Table II.2 shows the top 20 places of origin of all the international students enrolled in higher education programs in the U.S., for the period 2006/7 to 2009/10. Up to 2008/9, India, China, and South Korea, in that order, took the first 3 places, all seeing dramatic annual increases in numbers. But China was gaining on India's lead every year, and in 2009/10 overtook India to reach the top of the table with a mighty leap of 29.9 percent, while India's numbers increased by just 1.6 percent. Other countries sending more students in 2009/10 were Saudi Arabia (numbers up 24.9 percent, ranking up from 10th to 7th), Nigeria (up 5 percent), France (up 4 percent and one place), Vietnam, Turkey, the United Kingdom (up 1.8 percent and two places), and Brazil. Meanwhile, South Korea's numbers fell by 3.9 percent; so did the numbers coming from 10 other places of origin in 2008/9's top 20: Canada, Taiwan, Japan (the biggest faller), Mexico, Nepal, Germany, Thailand, Hong Kong, Indonesia, and Colombia.

Over the four years shown, the places of origin whose rankings improved included China, Canada (up 2 places to 4th), Saudi Arabia (up 5 places), Vietnam (up 11 places), Nepal (up 2 places), Brazil (up 2 places), and France (up 1 place). Kenya left the top 20. Japan, Mexico, Turkey, Germany, the United Kingdom, Hong Kong, and Colombia drifted down a place or two; Indonesia and Thailand drifted rather more.

TABLE II.2: TOP 20 SENDING PLACES OF ORIGIN FOR INTERNATIONAL UNIVERSITY AND
COLLEGE STUDENTS, 2006/07–2009/10

COUNTRY	2006/7	COUNTRY	2007/8	COUNTRY	2008/9	COUNTRY	2009/10 (% CHANGE)
1 India	83,833	India	94,563	India	103,260	China	127,628(+29.9)
2 China	67,723	China	81,127	China	98,235	India	104,897(+1.6)
3 South Korea	62,392	South Korea	69,124	South Korea	75,065	Korea	South 72,153 (-3.9)
4 Japan	35,282	Japan	33,974	Canada	29,697	Canada	28,145 (-5.2)
5 Taiwan	29,094	Canada	29,051	Japan	29,264	Taiwan	26,685 (-4.9)
6 Canada	28,280	Taiwan	29,001	Taiwan	28,065	Japan	24,842 (-15.1)
7 Mexico	13,826	Mexico	14,837	Mexico	14,850	Saudi Arabia	15,810 (+24.9)
8 Turkey	11,506	Turkey	12,030	Turkey	13,263	Mexico	13,450 (-9.4)
9 Thailand	8,886	Saudi Arabia	9,873	Vietnam	12,823	Vietnam	13,112 (+2.3)
10 Germany	8,656	Thailand	9,004	Saudi Arabia	12,661	Turkey	12,397 (+2.0)
11 United Kingdom	8,438	Nepal	8,936	Nepal	11,581	Nepal	11,233 (-3.0)
12 Saudi Arabia	7,886	Germany	8,907	Germany	9,679	Germany	9,548 (-1.4)
13 Nepal	7,754	Vietnam	8,769	Brazil	8,767	United Kingdom	8,861 (+1.8)
14 Hong Kong	7,722	United Kingdom	8,367	Thailand	8,736	Brazil	8,786 (+0.2)
15 Indonesia	7,338	Hong Kong	8,286	United Kingdom	8,701	Thailand	8,531 (-2.3)
16 Brazil	7,126	Indonesia	7,692	Hong Kong	8,329	Hong Kong	8,034 (-3.5)
17 Colombia	6,750	Brazil	7,578	Indonesia	7,509	France	7,716 (+4.0)
18 France	6,704	France	7,050	France	7,421	Indonesia	6,943 (-7.5)
19 Kenya	6,349	Colombia	6,662	Colombia	7,013	Colombia	6,920 (-1.3)
20 Vietnam	6,036	Nigeria	6,222	Nigeria	6,256	Nigeria	6,568 (+5.0)

Source: Chow, P. and Bhandari, R. (2010). Open doors 2010: Report on international
educational exchange. *New York: Institute of International Education*

Table II.3: Top 20 Sending Places of Origin for University and College Students by Level (2009/10)

	Undergraduate	Number	Graduate	Number	Non-degree	Number
1	China	39,921	India	68,290	China	10,251
2	South Korea	36,234	China	66,453	South Korea	6,671
3	India	15,192	South Korea	23,386	Japan	4,321
4	Canada	13,607	Taiwan	14,613	Saudi Arabia	3,247
5	Japan	13,063	Canada	11,950	Germany	2,379
6	Vietnam	8,864	Turkey	6,585	France	1,981
7	Saudi Arabia	8,767	Japan	5,390	Taiwan	1,894
8	Mexico	7,715	Thailand	4,553	India	1,758
9	Nepal	7,209	Mexico	3,911	United Kingdom	1,457
10	Taiwan	6,609	Saudi Arabia	3,474	Vietnam	1,278
11	Hong Kong	5,629	Germany	3,401	Mexico	1,044
12	Indonesia	4,313	Iran	3,773	Turkey	989
13	United Kingdom	4,217	Brazil	3,121	Spain	951
14	Malaysia	4,097	Colombia	3,113	Brazil	882
15	Brazil	4,083	Nepal	2,897	Italy	774
16	Turkey	3,656	France	2,639	Australia	714
17	Nigeria	3,498	United Kingdom	2,509	Colombia	631
18	Kenya	3,354	Vietnam	2,454	Thailand	621
19	Germany	3,213	Nigeria	2,327	Canada	619
20	Venezuela	2,780	Pakistan	2,157	Sweden	499

Source: Chow, P. and Bhandari, R. (2010). Open doors 2010: Report on international educational exchange. *New York: Institute of International Education.*

As table II.3 shows, however, the leading places of origin vary according to academic level. China achieved its top overall ranking in 2009/10 by sending many more undergraduates and non-degree students than India, but India (3rd for undergraduates and 8th for non-degree students) still led the graduates' table. South Korea, 3rd overall, was 2nd in the rankings for undergraduates and non-degree students. Taiwan, Turkey, and Thailand ranked higher in the graduates' table than in others; Iran appeared only in the graduates' top 20. Canada ranked 4th overall for undergraduates and 5th for graduates, but only 19th for non-degree students. Spain, Italy, and Australia appeared only in the non-degree top 20. Japan, Saudi Arabia, France, Germany, and the United Kingdom ranked higher in this table than in others. Places of origin that ranked highest for undergraduates, or only appeared in the undergraduates' top 20, include Vietnam, Mexico, Nepal, Hong Kong, Indonesia, Malaysia, Nigeria, Kenya, and Venezuela (which ranks 24th overall and has increased its numbers of tertiary students in the U.S. by 11.5 percent since 2007/8, including a 6 percent rise since 2008/9).

Table II.4 gives the numbers of international students enrolled in 2009/10 in each field of study, each study field's share of total international students, and each study field's share of international undergraduate students, graduate students, non-degree students and students on optional practical training. Business and management was the most popular field for international students, followed by engineering (except at the graduate level, where the order is reversed). Physical and life sciences ranked 3rd overall and at the graduate level, but lower at the undergraduate level. Math and computer science was the 4th most popular field overall, the 4th most popular at the undergraduate level, and the 3rd most popular for OPT, but ranked lower at the undergraduate level.

The 2009/10 figures for total numbers (all levels) in each field show that, compared to 2008/9, more international students were enrolled in business and management (up 5 percent), engineering (up 7.1 percent), math and computer science (up 7.8 percent), social sciences (up 4.4 percent), fine and applied arts (up 2.7 percent), education (up 1 percent), and agriculture (up 15.1 percent). Fewer were enrolled in physical and life sciences (down 0.7 percent), health professions (down 8.4 percent), intensive English language courses (down 8.6 percent), and humanities (down 6.2 percent). Business and management and fine and applied arts are most popular at the undergraduate level; engineering, education, agriculture, and physical and life sciences at the graduate level; intensive English language at the non-degree level; and math and computer science for OPT.

Open Doors 2010 tells us that in 2009/10, 55 percent of international tertiary students coming to the U.S. were male and 45 percent female—whereas 20 years earlier the ratio was 66:34. NAFSA: Association of International Educators estimated that international tertiary students contributed $18.8 billion to the U.S. economy in 2009/10; the Bureau of Economic Analysis of the U.S. Department of Commerce estimated $19.9 billion in 2009.

TABLE II.4: INTERNATIONAL STUDENTS IN THE U.S. BY FIELDS OF STUDY AND LEVEL (2009/10)

FIELD OF STUDY	NUMBER	% OF ALL	% OF UNDER-GRADUATE	% OF GRADUATE	% OF NON-DEGREE	% OF OPT
Business & Management	145,514	21.1	28.2	16.3	11.2	21.7
Engineering	127,441	18.4	12.9	24.8	3.8	23.7
Physical & Life Sciences	61,285	8.9	6.2	12.4	1.7	8.6
Social Sciences	59,865	8.7	9.3	9.0	3.7	7.2
Math & Computer Science	60,780	8.8	5.7	12.0	1.6	13.7
Health Professions	32,111	4.6	4.6	5.0	2.1	4.2
Fine & Applied Arts	35,801	5.2	6.6	4.4	2.7	5.1
Intensive English Language	26,075	3.8	1.1	0.0	42.7	2.6
Humanities	17,985	2.6	1.5	3.5	3.5	2.1
Education	18,299	2.6	1.4	4.1	1.1	1.8
Agriculture	10,317	1.5	0.8	2.1	0.7	1.4
Other Fields	76,743	11.1	16.9	6.2	15.2	7.4
Undeclared	18,707	2.7	4.8	0.2	10.0	0.5
Total	**671,616**	**100**	**100**	**100**	**100**	**100**

Source: Chow, P. and Bhandari, R. (2010). Open doors 2010: Report on international educational exchange. *New York: Institute of International Education.*

Section C

Exchange Visitors coming to the U.S. for education-related purposes

The Exchange Visitor program has 15 categories and several sub-categories. Eleven of the 15 categories, plus 4 sub-categories, have been classified as education-related for the purposes of this study because they are intended for students or include an education component. Visas for these 15 categories and sub-categories allow varying lengths of stay in the United States.

Table II.5 sets out the relevant visa categories and sub-categories, showing which visitors they cater to, the maximum duration of the visa, and the 12 Exchange Visitor scheme groups analyzed in this report.

For Exchange Visitors, or J-1 visa holders, information is recorded by the U.S. Department of State on the basis of those participating in a given year, rather than those enrolled at a given point in time. Moreover, statistics are collected according to the year in which individuals' participation in their Exchange Visitor scheme ends, not the year it began, which for some categories could have been some years earlier. And there have been some changes in categories over time. The Intern category was added in 2007 (in 2006 interns were classified as trainees), and Student Interns became a separate sub-category of College and University Undergraduate Students in 2009.

In the rest of this section, J-1 visa holders will be analyzed in "scheme groups." As table II.1 showed, the scheme groups chosen for this analysis are not exactly the same as the J-1 visa categories. A few categories that do not seem related to education have been removed; some others have been combined to give a clearer picture (i.e., to clarify if they have small numbers or have been merged or unmerged over time).

According to U.S. Department of State statistics, Exchange Visitors completing education-related programs in the last four years totaled 294,205 in 2006; rose to 324,299 in 2007; rose again to 330,185 in 2008; and plunged to 269,213 in 2009 as the global recession hit.

Table II.5: Education-Related Exchange Visitor (J-1) Visa Categories 2009

Visa Category/ Sub-category	Who for?	Max Length	Scheme Group used for this analysis
Au Pair	Individuals aged 18–26 entering the U.S. to live with an American host family, provide limited childcare services and attend some classes at an accredited U.S. postsecondary institution.	1 year, extendable	Au Pair
Camp Counselor	Individuals selected to be counselors in accredited U.S. summer camps, who impart skills and information about their country or culture.	4 months	Camp Counselor
College and University Student: Bachelor's	Individuals pursuing a full course of study for a bachelor's degree at accredited U.S. postsecondary educational institutions. Academic training is also permitted, but study must be the primary purpose. Students must have funding from own government or scholarships.	Depends on length of study program	Student, Under-graduate
College and University Student: Master's	Individuals pursuing a full course of study for a master's degree at accredited U.S. postsecondary educational institutions. Other conditions as for bachelor's.	As for bachelor's	Student, Graduate
College and University Student: Doctorate	Individuals pursuing a full doctorate at accredited U.S. postsecondary educational institutions. Other conditions as for bachelor's.	As for bachelor's	Student, Graduate
College and University Student: Non-degree	Individuals pursuing a full course of non-degree study at accredited U.S. postsecondary educational institutions. Other conditions as for bachelor's.	2 years	Student, Non-degree
College and University Student: Student Intern	Individuals pursuing internship programs at accredited U.S. post-secondary educational institutions. Other conditions as for bachelor's.	Depends on length of internship program	Student, Under-graduate
Intern	Individuals pursuing studies in a degree- or certificate-granting postsecondary academic institution outside the U.S., or who have graduated from such an institution in the previous 12 months, wishing to receive training in U.S. business practices and enhance skills in their chosen field (if it is in one of the U.S. approved list of fields)	12 months	Intern
Professor	Individuals engaged primarily in teaching, lecturing, observing, or consulting at accredited postsecondary academic institutions, museums, libraries, etc. They may also conduct research and participate in occasional lectures if authorized.	5 years (exceptions for certain federally funded programs)	Professor/ Teacher
Research Scholar	Individuals whose primary purpose is to conduct research, observe, or consult in connection with a research project at research institutions, corporate research facilities, museums, libraries, postsecondary accredited academic institutions, or similar. They may also teach or lecture, if permitted by their sponsor.	As for Professor	Research Scholar
Secondary School Student	Foreign secondary school students studying at a U.S. accredited public or private secondary school, living with an American host family.	One academic year	Secondary School Student
Short-term Scholar	Professors, research scholars, or similar, on short-term visits for the purpose of lecturing, observing, consulting, training, or demonstrating special skills at research institutions, museums, libraries, postsecondary accredited academic institutions, or similar.	6 months	Short-term Scholar

Source: U.S. Department of State information on J-1 visas supplied to the authors.

SCHEME GROUP	2006	2006%	2007	2007%	2008	2008%	2009	2009%
Summer work/ travel	129,211	43.92%	150,806	46.50%	153,369	46.45%	101,306	37.63%
Student: Non-degree	17,623	5.99%	20,811	6.42%	25,232	7.64%	29,081	10.80%
Student: Secondary	29,857	10.15%	29,446	9.08%	28,695	8.69%	27,589	10.25%
Research scholar	27,812	9.45%	25,965	8.01%	25,486	7.72%	26,370	9.80%
Camp counselor	20,694	7.03%	21,213	6.54%	21,483	6.51%	18,353	6.82%
Short-term scholar	11,916	4.05%	16,976	5.23%	18,561	5.62%	18,106	6.73%
Intern			1,851	0.57%	16,955	4.94%	14,501	5.39%
Au pair	15,673	5.33%	17,130	5.28%	16,306	5.14%	13,533	5.03%
Trainee	28,163	9.57%	27,164	8.38%	10,885	3.30%	7,800	2.90%
Student: Graduate	4,994	1.70%	5,012	1.55%	5,459	1.65%	5,738	2.13%
Student: Undergraduate	3,201	1.09%	3,111	0.96%	3,945	1.15%	3,995	1.48%
Professor/ teacher	5,061	1.72%	4,814	1.48%	3,809	1.19%	2,841	1.06%

Table II.6 shows how many visitors participated in (i.e., completed) education-related programs under each J-1 visa scheme group from 2006–09. Chart II.2 illustrates the proportion of visitors contributed by each scheme group in 2009.

- It will be seen that **Summer Work/Travel** accounted for more than two of every five Exchange Visitors completing education-related programs in 2006–08. Although this scheme fell below 40 percent in 2009, it is still by far the largest.

- **Secondary Students** contributed the next biggest numbers in 2006–08, but by 2009 had been overtaken by tertiary **Non-degree Students**.

- **Research Scholars**, **Camp Counselors**, and **Short-term Scholars**, in that order, took the next three places in all four years, though the Short-term Scholars are closing the gap with Camp Counselors, in percentage terms at least.

- **Au Pairs** made up over 5 percent of the visitors in every year, but the popularity of this scheme seems to be declining slightly.

- **Graduate Student** numbers rose every year. Numbers of **Undergraduate Students** have been moving upwards since 2007, and in 2009 they overtook **Professors/Teachers**, whose numbers are going down.

- **Trainee** numbers and percentages are also moving down, even if the **Intern** category introduced in 2007 is added to them.

CHART II.2: NUMBERS OF EDUCATIONAL EXCHANGE VISITORS TO U.S., BY GROUP, 2009

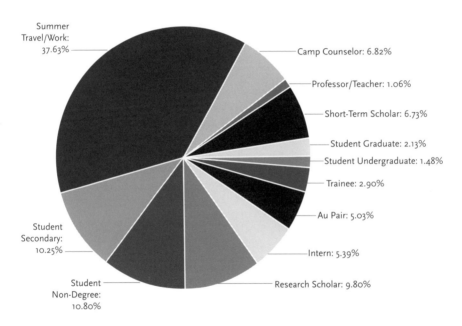

Source: U.S. Department of State information on J-1 visas supplied to the authors.

Mobility by group: Exchange Visitors (educational purposes)

We have analyzed the U.S. Department of State statistics for the education-related J-1 visa categories, by region and citizenship country. Our allocation of countries to regions is based on UNESCO's classification; it is not identical to that used by the U.S. Department of State in its own analyses. Appendix A shows our country breakdown by region. An important point to note is that in our classification, Europe includes Russia and Turkey, two big sending countries partly in Asia, as well as a number of small countries or territories that are administered by European countries, despite their geographical location in other regions.

Chart II.3 shows how many visitors completed education-related programs under each J-1 visa scheme group, by region, by year for 2006–09. It will be seen that every year Europe contributed the largest numbers, followed by Asia, South America, and other parts of North America. Every continent except Oceania saw its numbers rise from 2006–07. However, while numbers from Asia, South America, North America, and Africa rose again in 2008, numbers from Europe dipped in 2008 and even more in 2009. All regions except Oceania dipped somewhat from 2008–09, and only Asia sent higher numbers to the U.S. in 2009 than it had in 2006.

CHART II.3: NUMBERS OF EDUCATIONAL EXCHANGE
VISITORS TO U.S. BY REGION, BY YEAR (2006-2009)

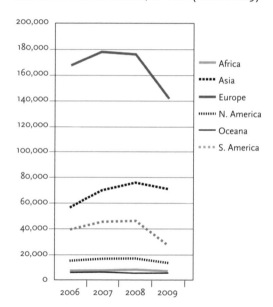

Source: U.S. Department of State information on J-1 visas supplied to the authors.

Chart II.4 shows the top 20 sending countries for U.S. Educational Exchange Visitors in 2009. As this chart shows, China was the top sending country for Exchange Visitors completing their participation in 2009, as well as for Student Visitors enrolled in 2009/10.

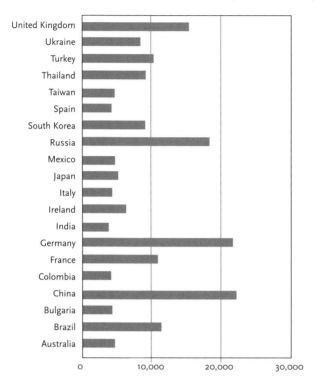

Source: U.S. Department of State information on J-1 visas supplied to the authors.

Table II.7 shows the top 20 countries and their numbers of participating students in the years 2006–09. This table shows some interesting changes over the period. From 2006–08, the top three sending countries were Russia, Germany, and Brazil, each increasing its numbers every year in line with world trends; while the UK occupied either 5th or 4th place. But in 2009, all these countries were overtaken by China. China has steadily increased its ranking and numbers every year: from 6th in 2006 with 11,042, to 5th in 2007 with 15,289, to 4th (overtaking the UK) in 2008 with 19,158, to a table-topping 22,247 in 2009, even as many other countries were falling back.

TABLE II.7: EDUCATIONAL EXCHANGE VISITORS: TOP 20 SENDING PLACES OF ORIGIN (2006–2009)

COUNTRY	2006	COUNTRY	2007	COUNTRY	2008	COUNTRY	2009
1 Russia	26,351	Russia	27,360	Russia	29,522	China	22,247
2 Germany	21,762	Germany	23,149	Germany	23,557	Germany	21,736
3 Brazil	17,068	Brazil	19,450	Brazil	19,897	Russia	18,319
4 Poland	15,544	United Kingdom	16,089	China	19,158	United Kingdom	15,402
5 United Kingdom	15,254	China	15,289	United Kingdom	16,363	Brazil	11,396
6 China	11,042	Poland	12,437	Turkey	12,478	France	10,871
7 France	9,914	Thailand	12,326	Thailand	11,224	Turkey	10,308
8 South Korea	9,469	France	10,546	France	11,193	Thailand	9,185
9 Bulgaria	9,351	Bulgaria	9,732	Ukraine	10,886	South Korea	9,119
10 Thailand	8,833	South Korea	9,488	South Korea	9,414	Ukraine	8,494
11 Ireland	7,334	Turkey	8,874	Ireland	8,851	Ireland	6,351
12 Peru	6,791	Ukraine	8,719	Peru	7,530	Japan	5,158
13 Romania	6,552	Ireland	7,821	Bulgaria	7,156	Mexico	4,835
14 Turkey	6,390	Peru	7,779	Colombia	6,265	Australia	4,724
15 Ukraine	6,173	Romania	6,033	Poland	5,961	Taiwan	4,700
16 Slovakia	6,053	Japan	5,862	Moldova	5,948	Bulgaria	4,358
17 Japan	5,887	Colombia	5,780	India	5,381	Spain	4,318
18 Canada	5,189	Moldova	5,600	Mexico	5,370	Italy	4,311
19 Australia	4,882	Mexico	5,070	Japan	5,358	Colombia	4,179
20 Colombia	4,713	Canada	4,989	Argentina	4,726	India	3,854

Source: U.S. Department of State information on J-1 visas supplied to the authors

Unsurprisingly, the changes in the top 20 countries over the period broadly parallel the trends in regional mobility in chart II.3. Chart II.3 shows numbers from Europe and South America dipping sharply in 2009, with only a slight decline in numbers from Asia. Had Russia and Germany been able to maintain in 2009 the numbers they sent in the two previous years, China would not have seized the top place. Germany and the UK at least sent roughly the same numbers in 2009 as in 2006 (the UK sent very slightly more), whereas Russia dropped from a top-ranking 26,351 in 2006 to a third-placed 18,319 in 2009, and Brazil sank from a third-placed 17,068 to a fifth-placed 11,396. Poland, which took 4th place in 2006, sent progressively fewer of its citizens to the U.S. as European Union membership opened up educational opportunities nearer home, dropping to 6th in 2007, 15th in 2008, and right out of the top 20 in 2009, by which time its numbers had fallen to 3,729, just 24 percent of 2006 numbers.

Places of origin that, like China, had higher rankings and higher numbers in 2009 than in 2006 included France (up one place and 10 percent), Thailand (up 2 places and 4 percent), Turkey (up 7 places and 61 percent), Ukraine (up 5 places and 38 percent), Mexico (up 8 places and 5 percent), Taiwan (up 18 places and 82 percent), Spain (up 7 places and 15 percent), Italy (up 5 places and 7 percent), and India (up 5 places and 13 percent). Places of origin that, like Russia, Brazil, and Poland, had lower rankings and lower numbers in 2009 than in 2006 included South Korea (down only one place and 4 percent), Peru (down 11 places and 50 percent), Canada (down 4 places and 31 percent), and three European countries whose citizens' interest in U.S. placements declined for the same reasons as in Poland: Bulgaria (down 7 places and 53 percent), Romania (down 22 places and 70 percent), and Slovakia (down 21 places and 69 percent).

Mobility by group: Au Pairs

The Au Pair scheme had 15,673 participants in 2006; 17,130 in 2007; 16,306 in 2008; and 13,533 in 2009, all under Exchange Visitor arrangements. In all these years, the largest numbers came from Europe, followed by South America, Asia, North America, Africa, and Oceania.

Table II.8 shows the scheme's top 20 sending countries in 2006–09. The Au Pair scheme's numbers fell more than most in 2009, dropping by 17 percent in a year. It shared this fate with some of the other short-duration schemes—those with a normal maximum stay of 12 months or less—particularly Summer Work/Travel (34 percent down) and Camp Counselors (15 percent down). These drops may simply reflect the fact that U.S. Department of State statistics are collected by year of program end rather than start, meaning that the effect of the global recession shows up sooner on the shorter schemes; these may also be the first to recover. It may be significant that Au Pair numbers also fell between 2007 and 2008, when total numbers rose—but so did the numbers in the Summer Work/Travel category.

Table II.8: Au Pairs (Exchange Visitors): Top 20 Sending Places of Origin (2006–2009)

Country	2006	Country	2007	Country	2008	Country	2009
1 Germany	3,729	Germany	4,651	Germany	4,820	Germany	3,931
2 Brazil	2,029	Brazil	2,267	Brazil	2,513	Brazil	1,747
3 Thailand	915	Thailand	1,118	Thailand	999	Sweden	866
4 Sweden	786	Sweden	947	Sweden	914	Colombia	761
5 Mexico	751	Mexico	840	Mexico	863	France	660
6 South Africa	676	Africa	632	Colombia	797	Mexico	620
7 France	586	France	580	France	690	Thailand	560
8 Poland	547	Colombia	519	South Africa	488	South Africa	512
9 Colombia	451	Poland	447	Austria	425	Austria	378
10 Czech Republic	345	Ukraine	420	Ukraine	389	Ukraine	288
11 Austria	337	Austria	394	Poland	250	China	249
12 Ecuador	316	Russia	281	China	192	Australia	183
13 Ukraine	299	Czech Republic	240	Panama	192	Poland	158
14 Romania	244	Ecuador	230	Russia	174	Czech Republic	152
15 Costa Rica	226	Panama	218	Costa Rica	172	Turkey	134
16 Bosnia & Herzegovina	226	Peru	208	Finland	159	Denmark	133
17 Panama	210	Costa Rica	188	Czech Republic	159	Panama	125
18 Russia	195	Bosnia & Herzegovina	186	Australia	147	Finland	122
19 Australia	192	Australia	175	Turkey	145	Argentina	119
20 Peru	170	Japan	139	Argentina	135	Japan	102

Source: U.S. Department of State information on J-1 visas supplied to the authors.

The Au Pairs top 20 list was headed consistently by Germany and Brazil in every year from 2006 to 2009. Of the top 20 countries in 2009, only Japan and Denmark were not also listed in 2008, and they were not far off. Over the period 2006–09, the most dramatic upward mover has been China, which ranked 50 in 2006. Countries that were in the top 20 in one or more of the earlier years but absent in 2009 included Costa Rica (21st in 2009), Russia (24th), the UK (30th), Bosnia and Herzegovina (36th), Peru (44th), Romania (50th), and Ecuador (59th). Countries that regularly rank just outside the top 20 include Bolivia, Chile, South Korea, Switzerland, and Norway.

Mobility by group: Camp Counselors

20,694 young people came to the U.S. as Camp Counselors in 2006; 21,213 in 2007; 21,483 in 2008; and 18,353 in 2009—all under J-1 visa arrangements. The 15 per-cent fall in Camp Counselor numbers in 2009 has already been mentioned, but unlike the Au Pair scheme, the Camp Counselor scheme did not lose numbers between 2007 and 2008, and in 2009 its share of all visitors for educational purposes rose slightly. The largest numbers came from Europe, followed by Oceania, Asia, North America, South America, and Africa. The last two regions had virtually equal numbers in 2009: African numbers were higher than South American in 2006 and 2007, lower in 2008. Table II.9 shows the top 20 places of origin sending Camp Counselors to the U.S. in the last four years.

Unsurprisingly, English-speaking places of origin dominate the Camp Counselors top 20 sending countries. The top six—the United Kingdom, Australia, Israel, Canada, New Zealand, and South Africa—remained in the same positions throughout 2006–09, except for a place swap between Canada and Israel in 2007. Overall, the top 20 places of origin are remarkably stable: none has been placed lower than 22nd at any time during the four-year period. The main dropout, Russia, ranked 15th in 2006, 20th in 2007, 22nd in 2008, and 23rd in 2009. Other places of origin that consistently appear in the top 30, and occasionally in the top 20, are Ukraine (21st in 2009 and 2008, 15th in 2008, 17th in 2006), India (22nd in 2009), Denmark, China, Taiwan, and Argentina.

Mobility by group: Summer Work/Travelers

This is by far the biggest educational visitor scheme under J-1 arrangements (F-1 visas are not available), though it is also the scheme that suffered most from the global recession of 2009. Visitors that year fell by 34 percent, but still accounted for 37.7 per-cent of J-1 educational visitors. Under the Summer Work/Travel scheme, 129,211 young people came to the U.S. in 2006; 150,806 in 2007; 153,369 in 2008; and 101,306 in 2009.

The largest numbers came from Europe, followed by Asia, South America, North America, and Africa. Europe's numbers plummeted in 2009, as did South America's. Asia's numbers—below South America's until that year—dropped far less, remaining

TABLE II.9: CAMP COUNSELORS (EXCHANGE VISITORS): TOP 20 SENDING PLACES OF ORIGIN (2006–2009)

	COUNTRY	2006	COUNTRY	2007	COUNTRY	2008	COUNTRY	2009
1	United Kingdom	9,048	United Kingdom	9,856	United Kingdom	10,530	United Kingdom	9,588
2	Australia	2,438	Australia	2,267	Australia	2,304	Australia	2,133
3	Canada	1,741	Israel	1,823	Israel	1,762	Israel	1,468
4	Israel	1,708	Canada	1,424	Canada	1,131	Canada	902
5	New Zealand	820	New Zealand	872	New Zealand	843	New Zealand	723
6	South Africa	571	South Africa	493	South Africa	384	South Africa	353
7	Netherlands	345	Netherlands	369	Mexico	327	Ireland	323
8	Ireland	289	Germany	308	Netherlands	324	Mexico	293
9	Germany	255	Mexico	276	Ireland	317	Netherlands	257
10	South Korea	247	Ireland	271	Germany	313	Colombia	244
11	Mexico	246	Poland	235	Colombia	299	Germany	187
12	France	240	Colombia	231	France	261	France	171
13	Poland	212	France	204	Hungary	212	Brazil	131
14	Colombia	205	Brazil	169	Brazil	205	Poland	125
15	Russia	180	Ukraine	160	South Korea	186	Czech Republic	124
16	Sweden	180	Hungary	159	Sweden	133	Spain	114
17	Ukraine	152	Sweden	152	Czech Republic	132	Hungary	110
18	Czech Republic	128	South Korea	151	Spain	129	South Korea	95
19	Spain	127	Czech Republic	140	Poland	126	Sweden	78
20	Hungary	117	Russia	126	Jamaica	123	Jamaica	77

Source: U.S. Department of State information on J-1 visas supplied to the authors

TABLE II.10: SUMMER WORK/TRAVELERS (EXCHANGE VISITORS): TOP 20 SENDING PLACES OF ORIGIN (2006–2009)

	COUNTRY	2006	COUNTRY	2007	COUNTRY	2008	COUNTRY	2009
1	Russia	23,642	Russia	24,814	Russia	27,517	Russia	16,593
2	Poland	13,435	Brazil	11,778	Brazil	11,797	Turkey	7,730
3	Brazil	9,806	Poland	10,597	Turkey	9,940	Ukraine	7,197
4	Bulgaria	8,756	Bulgaria	9,365	Ukraine	9,485	Thailand	6,242
5	Peru	6,158	Thailand	8,826	Thailand	7,815	Brazil	5,120
6	Ireland	5,946	Ukraine	7,121	Ireland	7,483	Ireland	4,754
7	Thailand	5,505	Peru	6,969	Bulgaria	6,907	Bulgaria	4,155
8	Romania	5,503	Turkey	6,714	Peru	6,828	China	3,152
9	Slovakia	5,174	Ireland	6,488	Moldova	5,547	Peru	2,945
10	Turkey	4,728	Romania	5,521	Poland	4,580	Jamaica	2,905
11	Ukraine	4,550	Moldova	5,100	Kazakhstan	3,991	Moldova	2,742
12	Argentina	3,146	Slovakia	4,192	Colombia	3,826	Taiwan	2,700
13	Colombia	2,816	Colombia	3,798	Argentina	3,681	Poland	2,469
14	Chile	2,412	Kazakhstan	3,406	Romania	3,459	Kazakhstan	2,089
15	Czech Republic	2,183	Argentina	3,223	Jamaica	3,324	Colombia	2,006
16	Kazakhstan	2,097	Chile	2,957	Chile	2,851	Argentina	2,004
17	Dominican Republic	1,958	Czech Republic	2,191	Taiwan	2,646	Belarus	1,843
18	Lithuania	1,864	Jamaica	2,137	Serbia	2,472	Romania	1,632
19	Moldova	1,706	Serbia & Montenegro	2,048	Slovakia	2,209	Czech Republic	1,509
20	Belarus	1,664	Dominican Republic	1,759	China	2,097	Serbia	1,399

Source: U.S. Department of State information on J-1 visas supplied to the authors

above their 2007 level. The smaller numbers from North America and Africa also dropped less, while Oceania's actually rose.

Table II.10 shows this scheme's top 20 sending places of origin in 2006–09. Below Russia, which consistently leads the rankings by some margin, the Summer Work/Travel scheme's top 20 table is quite volatile. Some places of origin have moved upwards over the four-year period—Turkey from 10th to 2nd, Ukraine from 11th to 3rd, China from 33rd to 8th, Jamaica from 23rd to 10th, Taiwan from 27th to 12th. Turkey, Ukraine, and Thailand (up from 7th to 4th) pushed Brazil, which ranked 2nd in 2007 and 2008, down to 5th in 2009. Meanwhile, other countries—including several from the former Soviet bloc whose EU membership has opened up more work/travel opportunities closer to home—have gone down, such as Poland from 2nd to 13th, Romania from 8th to 18th, Bulgaria from 4th to 7th, and the Czech Republic from 15th to 19th. For the same reason, dropouts from the top 20 included Slovakia, which sank from 9th to 22nd over the period, and Lithuania, which went from 18th to 30th. Conversely, some former Soviet bloc countries that are not EU member states and have not featured in any other top 20s—such as Kazakhstan, Belarus, and Serbia—appear particularly keen to take up summer work/travel opportunities. Other dropouts from the top 20 over the period include Chile, which went from 14th in 2006 to 23rd in 2009, and the Dominican Republic, which went from 17th to 37th.

Mobility by group: Secondary School Students

Secondary School Students may come to the U.S. on either J-1 or F-1 visas. Chart II.1 shows 24,988 "active" students who hold F-1 visas in this category as of June 2010, but we have no data on their origins or how long they had been in the United States. As it seems likely that most Secondary School Students holding F-1 visas are in the U.S. because their parents are, and the J-1 visa limit of 12 months does not apply to them, we assume that F-1 visa-holding secondary students generally stay longer than a year. Therefore, J-1 visas cover a majority of the secondary students starting or completing their participation in any given year.

J-1 visa data suggest that the Secondary School Students scheme is relatively recession-proof, compared to other short-duration Exchange Visitor schemes. Though numbers have declined every year over the period, in 2009 the scheme had a marginally larger share of educational exchange visitors than it had had in 2006. 29,857 secondary students entered the U.S. under the scheme in 2006, with 29,446 doing so in 2007; 28,695 in 2008; and 27,589 in 2009. In 2009 the number of students participating in the scheme fell by just 4 percent.

Europe contributed by far the largest numbers to this scheme, and European numbers rose from 2008–09, while all other regions' numbers fell or remained static. The next largest numbers were from Asia, followed by South America, North America, Africa, and Oceania.

Country	2006	Country	2007	Country	2008	Country	2009
1 Germany	8,199	Germany	8,185	Germany	7,970	Germany	7,960
2 Brazil	2,547	Brazil	2,387	Brazil	2,388	Brazil	1,901
3 South Korea	2,122	South Korea	1,726	South Korea	1,585	China	1,275
4 Thailand	1,307	Thailand	1,298	China	1,325	Thailand	1,213
5 Japan	1,184	Japan	1,051	Thailand	1,292	South Korea	1,108
6 Italy	937	China	1,028	Japan	864	Norway	915
7 Norway	751	Italy	881	Norway	850	Italy	889
8 China	717	Norway	803	Italy	838	Spain	877
9 Sweden	642	Sweden	660	France	684	Japan	764
10 France	634	France	659	Denmark	636	Denmark	671
11 Mexico	602	Denmark	657	Sweden	615	France	665
12 Denmark	577	Spain	562	Spain	594	Sweden	623
13 Spain	500	Mexico	547	Mexico	485	Mexico	435
14 Russia	439	Vietnam	519	Czech Republic	414	Belgium	426
15 Colombia	410	Switzerland	427	Switzerland	409	Switzerland	421
16 Switzerland	384	Russia	405	Vietnam	394	Taiwan	409
17 Taiwan	381	Taiwan	392	Taiwan	388	Vietnam	386
18 Vietnam	374	Belgium	379	Slovakia	388	Slovakia	366
19 Ecuador	361	Finland	377	Finland	386	Russia	364
20 Netherlands	346	Slovakia	369	Russia	378	Austria	348

Source: U.S. Department of State information on J-1 visas supplied to the authors

Table II.11 shows the top 20 countries sending secondary students to the U.S. under the Exchange Visitor scheme in 2006–09.

Like the Au Pair scheme, the Secondary School Students' top 20 table is headed by Germany and Brazil. No top 20 country has ever been out of the top 30 in the period 2006–09. Strong upward movers have included China, which rose from 8th to 3rd and displaced South Korea, the traditional third-place holder; Spain, up from 12th to 8th; Belgium, up from 23rd to 14th; Slovakia, up from 24th to 18th; and Austria, up from 26th to 20th. Meanwhile, Japan has slipped from 5th to 9th, Sweden from 9th to 12th, and Russia from 14th to 19th.

There is likely to be an association between the places of origin ranking high for participation in the Secondary School Students scheme and those ranking high for undergraduate study in the U.S., because the former may be useful preparation for the latter. It will be seen that 11 of the places of origin in table II.11 above also rank in the top 20 table for undergraduates holding J-1 visas (table II.12). These places of origin are China, Germany, France, South Korea, Mexico, Japan, Spain, Thailand, Sweden, Taiwan, Italy, and Brazil. This is particularly true of Asian countries: of the six Asian countries in table II.11, only Vietnam is missing from the undergraduates' top 20, coming in at 23rd.

Mobility by group: College and University Students

The broad category of College and University Students covers three of our Exchange Visitor scheme groups: Undergraduate Students, Graduate Students, and Non-degree Students. *The student numbers quoted below are, as mentioned earlier, included in the overall numbers of College and University Students discussed in section B above.*

Undergraduate Students completing their participation in the Exchange Visitor scheme numbered 3,201 in 2006; 3,111 in 2007; 3,945 in 2008; and 3,995 in 2009. Most were working toward bachelor's degrees, with some student interns. These numbers are not large in comparison with some other Exchange Visitor groups and with the numbers of higher education students coming to the U.S. as Student Visitors. They are kept low by the J-1 visa condition that students be funded by their own governments or from scholarships, rather than being self-financed. The numbers of Undergraduate Students holding J-1 visas appear to follow their own trajectory. They went down between 2006 and 2007 when overall educational Exchange Visitor numbers were rising, and up between 2008 and 2009 when overall numbers were falling. However, people can stay on this J-1 visa scheme for much longer than they can stay on the schemes already discussed. The typical U.S. bachelor's degree lasts four years or more; individuals completing in 2009 could well have made their initial decision to come to the U.S. several years earlier.

TABLE II.12: UNDERGRADUATE STUDENTS (EXCHANGE VISITORS): TOP 20 SENDING PLACES OF ORIGIN (2006–2009)

COUNTRY	2006	COUNTRY	2007	COUNTRY	2008	COUNTRY	2009
1 China	438	China	524	China	884	China	997
2 Kazakhstan	334	Germany	302	Germany	302	Germany	416
3 Germany	253	United Kingdom	183	Norway	278	France	256
4 France	212	France	182	France	214	South Korea	185
5 Japan	185	Mexico	148	Dominican Republic	201	United Kingdom	147
6 United Kingdom	171	Japan	127	United Kingdom	143	Mexico	126
7 South Korea	149	South Korea	115	South Korea	137	Japan	113
8 Mexico	145	Kazakhstan	105	Mexico	123	Kazakhstan	87
9 Spain	79	Netherlands	99	Japan	113	Spain	86
10 Netherlands	76	Dominican Republic	97	Kazakhstan	93	Malaysia	81
11 Jamaica	64	Norway	74	Spain	82	Netherlands	77
12 Australia	62	Australia	68	Malaysia	72	Australia	75
13 Sweden	55	Spain	68	Australia	68	Thailand	72
14 Canada	52	Taiwan	57	Netherlands	64	Sweden	64
15 Brazil	51	Sweden	52	Sweden	62	Canada	61
16 Taiwan	50	Finland	50	Brazil	54	Taiwan	58
17 Israel	47	Malaysia	48	Italy	54	Italy	57
18 Singapore	43	Thailand	45	Ireland	45	Brazil	53
19 Finland	42	Brazil	41	Finland	45	Singapore	53
20 Austria	41	Italy	41	Thailand	45	Dominican Republic	47

Source: U.S. Department of State information on J-1 visas supplied to the authors

Table II.12 shows the top 20 sending places of origin for undergraduate students holding J-1 visas recorded in the years 2006–09. China topped the table and increased its numbers every year. Germany ranked 3rd in 2006 and 2nd from 2007–09, with the highest numbers in 2009. France and the UK were in the top 6 every year. South Korea, ranked 7th in 2006–08, rose to 4th in 2009. Others regularly in the top 10 included Mexico, Japan, and Kazakhstan. Spain and the Netherlands consistently featured in the middle of the top 20 table; Australia, Sweden, and Brazil in the lower half. The fastest riser in the top 20 was Malaysia, which went from 22nd in 2006 to 10th in 2009, more than doubling its numbers.

Like the overall undergraduate numbers, this top 20 list is influenced by differences in the ability of places of origin to satisfy their citizens' demand for higher education within the place and the relative prestige of studying at home vs. abroad. Additionally, Exchange Visitor visas depend on the willingness of the places of origin to sponsor their citizens through university education overseas and/or the availability of other scholarship schemes to their citizens. The Chinese government, for example, has well-established arrangements to finance study abroad at recognized universities. Kazakhstan has a presidential scholarship scheme that selects the brightest students for fully funded study in leading overseas universities.

Graduate Students are those studying for master's degrees or doctorates. More graduates than undergraduates come to the U.S. under the Exchange Visitor scheme—4,994 completed in 2006; 5,012 in 2007; 5,459 in 2008; and 5,738 in 2009—and the numbers have been rising from year to year. As for undergraduates, numbers are constrained by the visa requirement of government or scholarship funding, and we also need to account for the time lag between a student's decision to come to the U.S. and the end of his or her study program.

Table II.13 shows the top 20 sending places of origin for Graduate Students completing their Exchange Visitor programs in the years 2006–09. China tops the table in every year, Germany is 2nd or 3rd, and France is well up in the top 10; but in other respects there are big differences between the undergraduate and the graduate top 20 list. Turkey, 2nd in 2008 and 2009 on the graduate list, is not even in the top 20 in the undergraduates' table. Nor is Pakistan (5th for graduates in 2009), Indonesia (7th), Vietnam (8th), Chile (10th), Israel, Colombia, Jamaica, Egypt, India, or Russia. Conversely, a number of places of origin in the 2009 undergraduate top 20 list do not appear in the 2009 graduate-level list; these include the UK (5th for undergraduates), Japan (7th), Kazakhstan (8th), Malaysia (10th), the Netherlands, Australia, Sweden, Canada, Italy, Singapore, and the Dominican Republic. Demand for a U.S. master's degree or doctorate, and governmental willingness to sponsor students, appears to be particularly strong in countries that cannot offer high-quality opportunities at this level to all of their best students.

TABLE II.13: GRADUATE STUDENTS (EXCHANGE VISITORS): TOP 20 SENDING PLACES OF ORIGIN (2006–2009)

	COUNTRY	2006	COUNTRY	2007	COUNTRY	2008	COUNTRY	2009
1	China	545	China	533	China	602	China	746
2	Germany	278	Germany	302	Turkey	416	Turkey	452
3	Thailand	258	France	216	Germany	326	Germany	269
4	France	231	Pakistan	207	Thailand	228	France	208
5	Kazakhstan	192	Turkey	191	Pakistan	198	Pakistan	206
6	Mexico	171	Thailand	165	France	192	Thailand	182
7	India	171	Mexico	157	Mexico	178	Indonesia	148
8	Turkey	139	Indonesia	138	Indonesia	136	Vietnam	135
9	Pakistan	134	India	123	India	126	Mexico	123
10	Brazil	127	South Korea	116	Vietnam	119	Chile	123
11	Vietnam	123	Egypt	115	Chile	112	Israel	104
12	South Korea	116	Kazakhstan	104	Israel	110	South Korea	103
13	Indonesia	104	Brazil	103	South Korea	104	Colombia	95
14	Taiwan	95	Israel	97	Spain	98	Brazil	93
15	Israel	90	Vietnam	97	Brazil	92	Spain	90
16	Philippines	87	Spain	93	Colombia	89	Jamaica	89
17	Spain	85	Taiwan	90	Russia	85	Egypt	88
18	Colombia	74	Canada	85	Taiwan	83	India	84
19	Canada	72	Russia	83	Egypt	81	Russia	83
20	Russia	72	Chile	82	Kazakhstan	79	Taiwan	81

Source: U.S. Department of State information on J-1 visas supplied to the authors

TABLE II.14: NON-DEGREE STUDENTS (EXCHANGE VISITORS): TOP 20 SENDING PLACES OF ORIGIN (2006–2009)

COUNTRY	2006	COUNTRY	2007	COUNTRY	2008	COUNTRY	2009
1 France	1,858	China	2,251	China	3,240	China	3,917
2 Germany	1,717	France	2,124	France	2,501	France	2,755
3 China	1,432	Germany	1,873	Germany	2,181	Germany	2,361
4 South Korea	1,332	South Korea	1,437	South Korea	1,809	South Korea	2,143
5 United Kingdom	1,272	United Kingdom	1,236	United Kingdom	1,340	United Kingdom	1,521
6 Japan	1,119	Japan	1,139	Japan	1,203	Japan	1,290
7 Mexico	685	Mexico	837	Mexico	889	Mexico	826
8 Australia	579	Australia	688	Spain	712	Australia	822
9 Spain	574	Spain	673	Australia	709	Spain	811
10 Netherlands	494	Netherlands	500	Brazil	637	Italy	764
11 Italy	455	Turkey	498	Italy	622	Norway	645
12 Sweden	403	Italy	446	Netherlands	570	Turkey	634
13 Denmark	346	Taiwan	404	Turkey	542	Netherlands	631
14 Austria	296	Sweden	363	Taiwan	402	Brazil	591
15 Brazil	287	Denmark	358	India	384	Sweden	519
16 Norway	272	India	334	Sweden	370	Egypt	519
17 Russia	263	Russia	331	Austria	359	Taiwan	483
18 Ireland	231	Austria	304	Denmark	343	Austria	459
19 Canada	225	Brazil	289	Russia	338	India	449
20 Turkey	223	Ireland	270	Egypt	320	Denmark	429

Source: U.S. Department of State information on J-1 visas supplied to the authors

Non-degree Student numbers coming to the U.S. through the Exchange Visitor scheme have grown significantly and steadily over the period 2006–09, from 17,623 completing programs in 2006 to 20,811 in 2007; 25,232 in 2008; and 29,081 in 2009. This category includes students on intensive English language courses. Table II.14 shows the top 20 sending countries for Non-degree Students at colleges and universities completing their programs in these years. This table has remained remarkably stable since 2006. The top eight countries, almost invariably in the same order, have been China (ranked only 3rd in 2006 but 1st every year since, with dramatic annual increases in numbers), France, Germany, South Korea, the United Kingdom, Japan, Mexico, Australia, and Spain (which swapped positions in 2008 but swapped back in 2009). The top 20 countries in 2009 had all appeared in the table at least once before.

Mobility by group: Professors and Teachers

The number of college and university professors coming to the U.S. under Exchange Visitor arrangements to be college or university Professors or Teachers in schools have declined over the period 2006–09. J-1 visa statistics record the following number of Professors and Teachers who completed their participation: 5,061 in 2006 (2,278 Professors, 2,783 Teachers); 4,814 in 2007 (1,794 Professors, 3,020 Teachers); 3,809 in 2008 (1,548 Professors, 2,397 Teachers); and 2,841 in 2009 (1,369 Professors, 1,472 Teachers). It is not clear why the numbers in both groups have declined. The explanation might simply be an increasing tendency for professors and teachers taking up posts in U.S. educational establishments to do so on work visas rather than under academic exchange arrangements or increased opportunities in their own countries.

Table II.15 shows the top 20 sending places for professors and teachers holding J-1 visas who completed their programs in the years 2006–09. This scheme's top 20 table again shows the rise of China—leaping from 4th to 1st place in 2007 by increasing its numbers significantly even as other countries reduced theirs. Spain started in 1st place but drifted down to 3rd, more than halving its numbers over the period. France, whose numbers declined less steeply than Spain's, started the period in 3rd position but ended in 2nd. The Philippines, which was in 2nd position in 2006, had disappeared from the top 20 list by 2009, as had Romania, Jamaica, and Brazil. Other less dramatic downward movers during this period included India, the UK, and Canada. Places whose numbers rose in the table included Israel (from 18th to 9th), Mexico, Germany, South Korea, Colombia, Italy, Argentina, Russia, and Australia, though none of these increased their numbers. Turkey, Austria, and Taiwan joined the table for the first time in 2009; Uruguay joined for the first time in 2008.

TABLE II.15: PROFESSORS AND TEACHERS (EXCHANGE VISITOR SCHEME): TOP 20 SENDING PLACES OF ORIGIN (2006–2009)

COUNTRY	2006	COUNTRY	2007	COUNTRY	2008	COUNTRY	2009
1 Spain	554	China	515	China	579	China	511
2 Philippines	468	Spain	444	Spain	401	France	312
3 France	430	France	386	France	337	Spain	261
4 China	374	Philippines	324	India	215	Mexico	146
5 India	283	India	322	Mexico	206	Germany	116
6 United Kingdom	274	United Kingdom	217	United Kingdom	169	South Korea	114
7 Mexico	237	Mexico	199	Philippines	140	India	108
8 Germany	219	South Korea	164	Colombia	139	United Kingdom	81
9 South Korea	176	Colombia	159	Germany	133	Israel	71
10 Canada	155	Germany	156	South Korea	114	Colombia	62
11 Colombia	140	Canada	119	Canada	105	Italy	61
12 Romania	108	Jamaica	118	Jamaica	86	Turkey	60
13 Japan	107	Japan	82	Greece	74	Japan	53
14 Jamaica	104	Israel	79	Japan	70	Canada	52
15 Italy	102	Italy	78	Brazil	67	Argentina	50
16 Brazil	79	Romania	71	Italy	61	Russia	39
17 Russia	78	Brazil	69	Israel	58	Uruguay	35
18 Israel	77	Russia	67	Russia	50	Australia	33
19 Argentina	73	Argentina	65	Uruguay	49	Austria	32
20 Australia	61	Greece	57	Argentina	48	Taiwan	32

Source: U.S. Department of State information on J-1 visas supplied to the authors

Mobility by group: Research Scholars and Short-term Scholars

Whereas most Exchange Visitor schemes attracted their lowest numbers in 2006 and 2009, the numbers recorded for **Research Scholars** were highest in these years: 27,812 Research Scholars completed their programs in 2006; 25,965 in 2007; 25,486 in 2008; and 26,370 in 2009. As J-1 visa-holders, scholars in this category can remain for up to five years, but their decisions to come to the U.S. would have been taken some time earlier.

Table II.16 shows the top 20 sending places of origin for Research Scholars. The top 3 sending places of origin 2006–09 have consistently been China, South Korea, and Japan. China increased its numbers by a massive 64 percent over the period, while South Korea, Japan, and all other top 20 places of origin except India and Turkey reduced theirs. India rose to 4th place in 2008, displacing Germany. Italy, France, Brazil, and Spain have ranked from 6th to 9th in all four years; Taiwan, the UK, and Canada from 10th to 12th, but in varying order. Turkey, ranked 16th in 2006 and 13th in 2009, was the only place of origin other than China to send more Research Scholars to the U.S. every year. The new top 20 entrants over the period were Sweden and Switzerland; the dropouts were Poland, Australia, and Egypt.

Short-term Scholars' functions are similar to those of Research Scholars, but can remain in the U.S. only for six months. Because Research Scholars, in comparison, can stay for up to five years, it follows that many more of the Short-term Scholars will complete their programs in any given year. Short-term Scholar numbers rose steeply from 2006–08, falling back just a little in 2009. Short-term Scholars completed 11,916 programs in 2006; 16,976 in 2007; 18,561 in 2008; and 18,106 in 2009.

Table II.17 shows the top 20 sending places of origin for Short-term Scholars. China again dominated the top 20, increasing its numbers by 88 percent over the period. Germany, in 2nd position for all four years, sent only half as many scholars as China, but Germany's numbers rose by 89 percent from 2006–09. France was in 4th position, having held the 3rd and 4th spots since 2007. Italy rose from 6th in 2006 to 3rd in 2009, overtaking France. Upward movers in 2006–09 include Spain (7th to 5th), the UK (10th to 7th), South Korea (9th to 8th), Brazil (12th to 9th), the Netherlands (14th to 10th), and Japan (16th to 13th). India, Mexico, Canada, Poland, and Taiwan fell in the rankings despite recording net increases. Russia, 3rd in 2006, fell in both relative and absolute terms. Egypt (8th in 2006), Thailand, Ukraine, Azerbaijan, and Argentina made one or more appearances in the top 20 during the period, but had dropped out by 2009. Turkey and Israel joined the table in 2007, Indonesia in 2008, and Pakistan in 2009.

TABLE II.16: RESEARCH SCHOLARS (EXCHANGE VISITOR SCHEME): TOP 20 SENDING PLACES OF ORIGIN (2006–2009)

	COUNTRY	2006	COUNTRY	2007	COUNTRY	2008	COUNTRY	2009
1	China	4,832	China	6,410	China	6,709	China	7,912
2	South Korea	3,297	South Korea	3,300	South Korea	3,192	South Korea	2,968
3	Japan	2,038	Japan	1,855	Japan	1,690	Japan	1,574
4	Germany	1,733	Germany	1,378	India	1,358	India	1,399
5	India	1,327	India	1,363	Germany	1,238	Germany	1,289
6	Italy	1,314	France	1,038	France	981	Italy	1,018
7	France	1,303	Italy	943	Italy	947	France	977
8	Spain	935	Brazil	685	Brazil	705	Brazil	702
9	Brazil	825	Spain	671	Spain	677	Spain	634
10	United Kingdom	733	Taiwan	604	Taiwan	580	Taiwan	573
11	Taiwan	680	United Kingdom	537	Canada	500	United Kingdom	557
12	Canada	555	Canada	501	United Kingdom	479	Canada	460
13	Netherlands	488	Israel	408	Turkey	435	Turkey	450
14	Russia	474	Turkey	384	Israel	407	Israel	387
15	Israel	463	Russia	319	Mexico	304	Mexico	319
16	Turkey	380	Netherlands	309	Netherlands	301	Netherlands	289
17	Mexico	377	Mexico	284	Egypt	274	Thailand	245
18	Poland	323	Egypt	265	Russia	248	Russia	223
19	Australia	308	Thailand	239	Thailand	215	Sweden	195
20	Thailand	304	Poland	235	Greece	197	Switzerland	192

Source: U.S. Department of State information on J-1 visas supplied to the authors

TABLE II.17: SHORT-TERM SCHOLARS (EXCHANGE VISITOR SCHEME): TOP 20 SENDING PLACES OF ORIGIN (2006–2009)

COUNTRY	2006	COUNTRY	2007	COUNTRY	2008	COUNTRY	2009
1 China	1,482	China	2,351	China	2,695	China	2,792
2 Germany	725	Germany	1,154	Germany	1,320	Germany	1,370
3 Russia	548	France	813	France	932	Italy	944
4 France	449	Italy	708	Italy	921	France	885
5 India	426	South Korea	681	Spain	830	Spain	797
6 Italy	416	Spain	672	Brazil	699	India	600
7 Spain	404	Brazil	655	India	672	United Kingdom	566
8 Egypt	394	India	640	South Korea	593	South Korea	490
9 South Korea	391	United Kingdom	631	United Kingdom	562	Brazil	481
10 United Kingdom	308	Russia	578	Mexico	462	Netherlands	406
11 Mexico	300	Egypt	485	Russia	455	Russia	383
12 Brazil	265	Mexico	454	Netherlands	424	Mexico	378
13 Canada	200	Japan	340	Egypt	423	Japan	359
14 Netherlands	191	Taiwan	313	Canada	311	Canada	294
15 Poland	182	Canada	311	Japan	307	Israel	279
16 Japan	177	Netherlands	295	Taiwan	305	Indonesia	276
17 Thailand	163	Israel	267	Israel	282	Pakistan	272
18 Ukraine	156	Turkey	257	Turkey	252	Turkey	251
19 Taiwan	153	Poland	218	Poland	238	Poland	249
20 Azerbaijan	153	Argentina	164	Indonesia	205	Taiwan	233

Source: U.S. Department of State information on J-1 visas supplied to the authors

Mobility by group: Trainees and Interns

These groups are discussed under the same heading because, as explained earlier, the Exchange Visitor Intern category was added only in 2007; in 2006 Interns were classified as Trainees. In J-1 visa data, Trainees, Trainees (Specialty), and Trainees (Non-Specialty) are recorded separately, but in this report we have used the term Trainee for all three.

Since 2007, Intern numbers have gradually built up while Trainee numbers have declined, as shown in table II.18. The total combined numbers of Trainees and Interns rose slightly from 2006–07; fell back in 2008 below 2006 levels; and fell sharply from 2008–09. One possible explanation might be that international students, keen to improve their work-related skills and knowledge, are pursuing non-degree programs at colleges and universities instead, or pursuing internships in their home countries.

TABLE II.18: TRAINEES AND INTERNS (EXCHANGE VISITOR SCHEME): NUMBERS BY YEAR (2006–2009)

	2006	2007	2008	2009
TRAINEES	28,163	27,164	10,885	7,800
INTERNS	0	1,851	16,955	14,501
TOTAL	28,163	29,015	27,840	22,301

The Exchange Visitor scheme is of course not the only way for an international student to undertake training in the United States. As mentioned earlier, M-1 visas are available for some types of vocational training. As of June 30, 2010, there were some 7,000 "active" M-1 visa students, of whom 4,300 were pursuing flight training. But because of a lack of M-1 visa data that is comparable to our J-1 visa data, the following analysis must be confined to the much larger numbers of Trainees and Interns on the Exchange Visitor program.

Table II.19 shows the top 20 sending countries for Trainees. Table II.20 shows the top 20 sending countries for Interns from 2007–09, plus a 2009 top 20 list for Trainees and Interns combined.

From tables II.19 and II.20 we can see that the leading countries' participation in the Trainee/Intern schemes has followed quite a stable pattern over time. The top 5 countries in the Trainees table for 2006 and 2007—Germany, France, the UK, South Korea, and Canada, in that order—still take the top five places when Trainees and Interns are combined. Similarly, India ranks 6th and Japan (still sending an unusually large proportion of international students under the Trainee rather than the Intern

TRAINEES	2006	TRAINEES	2007	TRAINEES	2008	TRAINEES	2009
1 Germany	4,423	Germany	4,124	France	1,004	United Kingdom	725
2 France	3,065	France	3,219	India	865	France	701
3 United Kingdom	1,784	United Kingdom	1,755	United Kingdom	861	Japan	696
4 Canada	1,221	South Korea	1,257	Japan	764	Germany	523
5 South Korea	1,075	Canada	1,139	Germany	745	India	358
6 Brazil	936	India	1,092	China	447	China	347
7 Japan	829	Japan	969	South Korea	436	South Korea	300
8 China	788	Brazil	969	Brazil	331	Brazil	212
9 India	760	China	730	Italy	289	Turkey	207
10 Mexico	728	Mexico	637	Mexico	268	Mexico	190
11 Netherlands	624	Netherlands	555	Spain	256	Italy	187
12 Ireland	593	Ireland	538	Turkey	237	Spain	185
13 Italy	580	Italy	479	Philippines	208	Ireland	181
14 Ukraine	470	Australia	407	Norway	180	South Africa	176
15 Russia	446	Israel	366	South Africa	176	Ukraine	137
16 Australia	443	Spain	365	Ireland	172	Malaysia	131
17 Poland	442	Philippines	351	Australia	160	Australia	125
18 Switzerland	376	Ukraine	350	Canada	159	Thailand	121
19 Romania	366	Turkey	343	Netherlands	151	Argentina	116
20 Sweden	347	Sweden	332	Malaysia	132	Switzerland	113

Source: U.S. Department of State information on J-1 visas supplied to the authors

scheme) ranks 7th in the Combined table, as they did in the Trainee table for 2007. China, Brazil, Mexico, and the Netherlands have always been in or near the top 10. However, there are a few more changes in the bottom half of the top 20. As we have seen in other schemes, Turkey has risen up the rankings over the period, as have Ireland and Spain. South Africa and Thailand have joined the rankings since 2007; dropouts since 2006/7 include Poland, Romania, Israel, Switzerland, and Australia.

Table II.20: Top 20 Sending Countries for Interns (2007–09) and Combined Total for Trainees and Interns (2009)

Interns	2007	Interns	2008	Interns	2009	Combined total T + I	2009
1 Germany	489	Germany	4,019	Germany	3,147	Germany	3,670
2 France	169	France	2,456	France	2,316	France	3,017
3 South Korea	131	Canada	994	South Korea	1,411	South Korea	1,711
4 India	120	South Korea	955	Canada	756	United Kingdom	1,388
5 Canada	97	India	831	United Kingdom	663	Canada	849
6 United Kingdom	95	United Kingdom	765	Ireland	520	India	807
7 Netherlands	89	Netherlands	498	India	449	Japan	805
8 Peru	62	Mexico	420	Netherlands	418	Ireland	701
9 Mexico	62	Brazil	409	Mexico	356	China	655
10 Brazil	38	China	298	Brazil	335	Brazil	547
11 China	35	Ireland	292	China	308	Mexico	546
12 Switzerland	30	Spain	226	Spain	248	Netherlands	527
13 Spain	30	Austria	210	Sweden	195	Spain	433
14 Turkey	26	Sweden	209	Thailand	173	Turkey	352
15 Australia	24	Colombia	199	Colombia	171	Italy	327
16 Singapore	24	Turkey	191	Philippines	163	South Africa	301
17 Colombia	22	Switzerland	163	Ukraine	158	Ukraine	295
18 Sweden	22	Ukraine	148	Austria	156	Thailand	294
19 Austria	20	Peru	148	Turkey	145	Sweden	281
20 Italy	18	Italy	146	Italy	140	Philippines	269

Source: U.S. Department of State information on J-1 visas supplied to the authors

Conclusions

Our analysis of evidence for the period up to and including 2009 has shown that international students remain keen to come to the U.S. and take advantage of the many and varied educational opportunities the country can offer. Though the numbers coming on J-1 visas under Exchange Visitor arrangements (measured by the date individuals complete their programs) declined in 2009 after two very good years, the falls were mainly in the shorter, less obviously career-enhancing visitor categories (e.g., Summer Work/Travel, Camp Counselor, Au Pair). These categories, such as Professor/Teacher and Trainee/Intern, may have declined because these groups have decided to pursue other visa options. The demand for Exchange Visitor opportunities at the postsecondary level—on undergraduate, graduate, and non-degree programs—remains healthy.

Similarly, although the latest *Open Doors* figures (2009/10) show only limited growth in international students coming to the U.S. for college and university programs, new enrollments increased by 40 percent in the three years from 2005/6 to 2008/9. One lean year after several fat years does not necessarily herald a continuing downward trend.

There have been significant recent changes in the top sending regions and countries. In this field as in others, Asia's star is rising. In the latest year, China had more international students completing programs in the U.S. under Exchange Visitor arrangements than any other country—having topped the rankings for Undergraduates, Graduates, Non-degree Students, Research Scholars, Short-term Scholars, and Professors and Teachers, and risen rapidly up the rankings as a sender of Secondary School Students, Summer Work/Travelers, and even Au Pairs. China also overtook India to lead the sending table for international students enrolled in U.S. colleges and universities. India ranked 2nd in number of College and University Students studying in the U.S., and also ranked 20th for visitors sent under Exchange Visitor arrangements (4th for Research Scholars and 5th for Trainees). South Korea was the 3rd biggest sender of College and University Students, and ranked 9th for overall numbers sent under Exchange Visitor arrangements. Japan fell to 6th position for College and University Students, having sent lower numbers every year since 2005/6, but improved its position in the Exchange Visitor rankings to 12th (3rd for Research Scholars and Trainees). Taiwan overtook Japan for 5th position in numbers of College and University Students sent, and was 15th for Exchange Visitors. Thailand ranked 8th for Exchange Visitors and 15th for College and University Students. Newcomer Vietnam was ranked 9th for College and University Students and also a keen sender of Graduate and Secondary School Students under Exchange Visitor arrangements. Saudi Arabia (also in Asia under our classification) rose 3 places to rank 7th for College and University Students.

Europe still sends more Exchange Visitors than any other region, but its lead over Asia is narrowing and only four European countries appeared in the 2009/10 top 20 for college and university students. The largest countries of "old Europe" are still important senders. In the latest figures, Germany was the second largest sender under Exchange Visitor arrangements, leading the tables for Au Pairs, Secondary School Students, Interns, and Trainees and Interns combined; it also ranked 12th for College and University Students. The UK ranked 4th for sending Exchange Visitors, leading the tables for Camp Counselors and Trainees, and overtook Brazil and Thailand to rank 13th for College and University Students. France was 6th for Exchange Visitors (2nd for Professors/Teachers and Trainees and Interns) and rose one place to 17th position for College and University Students, overtaking Indonesia. Europe's fastest recent riser has been Turkey, which came 7th for sending Exchange Visitors (2nd for Graduates and Summer Work/Travelers) and 10th—the highest-placed European country—in numbers of college and university students in the United States. Ukraine is another riser in the Exchange Visitor category, ranking 10th (3rd for Summer Work/Travel). However, several Central and Eastern European countries that formerly sent significant numbers under Exchange Visitor schemes, including Poland, Bulgaria, Romania, and Slovakia, no longer do so. Russia, which sent the highest number of Exchange Visitors in the three years up to 2008, slipped to 3rd place in the latest rankings. Today, Russia leads only the table for Summer Work/Travelers, and does not rank among the top 20 sending countries for college and university students.

South America, the third largest sending region, has also seen its numbers fall in recent years. Brazil sends more international students than any other country in the region; it ranked 14th in 2009/10 for sending College and University Students. Brazil has slipped from 3rd to 5th position in the Exchange Visitor rankings over the last four years, though it still occupies 2nd position for Au Pairs and Secondary School Students. Colombia currently stands at 19th in the top 20 in both the College and University Students category and the Exchange Visitors category; it ranks 4th for sending Au Pairs. Peru, 12th for sending Exchange Visitors in 2008, has now left the top 20.

There have been fewer changes in the smaller sending regions. The biggest sending countries from North America are still Canada and Mexico. In the latest figures, Canada ranked 4th for college and university students but was not in the Exchange Visitors top 20, though it did come 4th for Camp Counselors and Trainees. Mexico ranked 8th for College and University Students, down one place in 2009/10, and 13th in the Exchange Visitors top 20 (4th for Professors/Teachers, 6th for Au Pairs). In Oceania, the only country to send significant numbers to the U.S. is Australia, which ranked 14th in the Exchange Visitors top 20 (2nd for Camp Counselors). The largest sending country in Africa, South Africa, did not make it into the top 20 for either Exchange Visitors or College and University Students, but ranked 6th for Camp Counselors and 8th for Au Pairs.

Appendix A
REGIONS USED IN U.S. COUNTRY STUDY
Places of origin listed in order of their total Exchange Visitor numbers, 2006–09

AFRICA

South Africa, Egypt, Ghana, Nigeria, Morocco, Kenya, Tunisia, Tanzania, Zimbabwe, Uganda, Cameroon, Senegal, Ethiopia, Libya, Malawi, Namibia, Zambia, Algeria, Cote D'Ivoire, Mali, Botswana, Rwanda, Congo (Democratic Republic of), Madagascar, Mauritius, Angola, Mozambique, Benin, Sudan, Burkina Faso, Sierra Leone, Congo, Liberia, Togo, Guinea, Niger, Lesotho, Cape Verde, Swaziland, Gabon, Mauritania, Gambia, Guinea-Bissau, Chad, Burundi, Eritrea, Central African Republic, Djibouti, Equatorial Guinea, Somalia, Comoros, Seychelles.

ASIA AND THE MIDDLE EAST

China, Thailand, South Korea, Japan, India, Taiwan, Kazakhstan, Israel, Philippines, Vietnam, Hong Kong, Singapore, Indonesia, Malaysia, Kyrgyzstan, Pakistan, Jordan, Azerbaijan, Uzbekistan, Mongolia, Georgia, Armenia, Tajikistan, Lebanon, Iran, Afghanistan, Turkmenistan, Bangladesh, Saudi Arabia, Nepal, Iraq, Sri Lanka, West Bank, Cambodia, Yemen, Syria, Oman, Kuwait, Burma, Bahrain, Macau, United Arab Emirates, Gaza Strip, Laos, Qatar, Bhutan, Timor-Leste, Maldives, Brunei, North Korea, British Indian Ocean Territory.

EUROPE

Russia, Germany, United Kingdom, France, Turkey, Poland, Ukraine, Bulgaria, Ireland, Romania, Moldova, Italy, Spain, Slovakia, Czech Republic, Sweden, Netherlands, Belarus, Norway, Denmark, Austria, Hungary, Serbia, Lithuania, Switzerland, Macedonia, Finland, Serbia and Montenegro, Belgium, Croatia, Portugal, Greece, Estonia, Bosnia and Herzegovina, Albania, Latvia, Slovenia, Montenegro, Cyprus, Iceland, Kosovo, Luxembourg, Malta, Liechtenstein, Andorra, Greenland, Monaco, Isle of Man, Reunion, San Marino, Jersey, French Polynesia, Netherlands Antilles, Martinique, Faroe Islands, French Guiana, New Caledonia, South Georgia and the South Sandwich Islands, Guernsey, Montserrat, Pitcairn Islands, Falkland Islands (Islas Malvinas), Guadeloupe, Jan Mayen, Saint Pierre and Miquelon.

NORTH AMERICA

Mexico, Canada, Jamaica, Dominican Republic, Costa Rica, Panama, Guatemala, El Salvador, Honduras, Haiti, Nicaragua, Trinidad and Tobago, Barbados, Belize, Bahamas, Antigua and Barbuda, Saint Lucia, Cuba, Grenada, Saint Vincent and the Grenadines, Dominica, Saint Kitts and Nevis, Bermuda, Cayman Islands, Anguilla, British Virgin Islands.

OCEANIA

Australia, New Zealand, Fiji, Papua New Guinea, Samoa, Tonga, Solomon Islands, Kiribati, Micronesia, Tuvalu, Christmas Island, Cook Islands, Vanuatu.

SOUTH AMERICA

Brazil, Peru, Colombia, Argentina, Chile, Ecuador, Venezuela, Paraguay, Bolivia, Uruguay, Suriname, Guyana, Aruba, Bovet Island.

OTHER

Unknown, stateless, neutral zone.

AUTHORS' NOTE

This study is an attempt to document as fully as possible the scale and range of global mobility for all educational purposes at the end of the first decade of the twenty first century.

Our first challenge was to assemble current information on this wide-ranging subject from as many sources as possible. We drew heavily on previous publications, especially those from OECD, UNESCO, and IIE (*Open Doors*, Atlas of Student Mobility, and previous IIE and AIFS Foundation Global Education Research Reports), and gathered data from many sources. Most of the data used in this book is publicly available, but some is not. We are especially indebted to Stanley Colvin and Susan Geary at the U.S. Department of State, who gave us unique access to comprehensive and previously unpublished statistics on educational mobility under the exchange visitor programs operated by the U.S. government.

The use made of this invaluable information, and any interpretations put on it, are entirely the authors' responsibility, as are any errors or omissions.

We are also grateful to many friends and colleagues who supplied us with relevant information or helped us to track it down, particularly Ian Whitman and Jean Yip of OECD, Jamil Salmi and Michael Crawford from the World Bank, international higher education consultant John Fielden, Francisco Marmolejo of CONAHEC, Adam Pokorny of the European Commission's Comenius Unit, Irina Lungu from the Academic Cooperation Association, and Peter Kerrigan and Simone Burkhart of DAAD.

We would also like to thank all those who attended a seminar in New York organized by IIE in November 2010 and gave us the benefit of their knowledge and expertise in commenting on our preliminary findings.

Finally, we are immensely grateful to Sir Cyril Taylor and Bill Gertz of the AIFS Foundation and Allan Goodman of IIE for commissioning our study, and to Peggy Blumenthal, Rajika Bhandari, Raisa Belyavina, Daniel Obst, and Luke Epplin at IIE for their patience, enthusiasm, and support.

BIBLIOGRAPHY

American Council on Education. (2009, September). *Sizing up the competition: The future of international postsecondary student enrollment in the United States.* ACE Issue Brief. Retrieved February 21, 2011 from www.acenet.edu

Association of Indian Universities (AIU) (2011). India. In R. Bhandari, R. Belyavina, & R. Gutierrez (Eds.), *Student mobility and the internationalization of higher education: National policies and strategies from six world regions—A Project Atlas® report.* (pp. 55-60). New York: Institute of International Education.

Aussie education market faces hard years. (January 11, 2011). *The Economic Times.* Retrieved March 4, 2011, from http://articles.economictimes.indiatimes.com/2011-01-11/news/28427330_1_student-visa-education-providers-student-numbers

Australian Education International (AEI) (2011). Australia. In R. Bhandari, R. Belyavina, & R. Gutierrez (Eds.), *Student mobility and the internationalization of higher education: National policies and strategies from six world regions—A Project Atlas® report* (pp. 113-118). New York: Institute of International Education.

Bhandari, R., Belyavina, R., & Gutierrez, R. (2011). *Student mobility and the internationalization of higher education: National Policies and strategies from six world regions—A Project Atlas® report.* New York: Institute of International Education.

Bhandari, R. & Chow, P. (2009). *Open doors 2009: Report on international educational exchange.* New York: Institute of International Education.

Bhandari, R. & Laughlin, S. (Eds.). (2009). *Higher education on the move: New developments in global mobility.* New York: Institute of International Education.

British Council (2011). United Kingdom. In R. Bhandari, R. Belyavina, & R. Gutierrez (Eds.), *Student mobility and the internationalization of higher education: National policies and strategies from six world regions—A Project Atlas® report* (pp. 105-111). New York: Institute of International Education.

CampusFrance (2011). France. In R. Bhandari, R. Belyavina, & R. Gutierrez (Eds.), *Student mobility and the internationalization of higher education: National policies and strategies from six world regions—A Project Atlas® report* (pp. 73-78). New York: Institute of International Education.

Canadian Bureau for International Education (CBIE). (2011). Canada. In R. Bhandari, R. Belyavina, & R. Gutierrez (Eds.), *Student mobility and the internationalization of higher education: National policies and strategies from six world regions—A Project Atlas® report* (pp. 25-30). New York: Institute of International Education.

Centre for International Mobility (CIMO) (2011). Finland. In R. Bhandari, R. Belyavina, and R. Gutierrez (Eds.), *Student mobility and the internationalization of higher education: National policies and strategies from six world regions—A Project Atlas® report* (pp. 69-72). New York: Institute of International Education.

China Scholarship Council (CSC) (2011). China. In R. Bhandari, R. Belyavina, & R. Gutierrez (Eds.), *Student mobility and the internationalization of higher education: National policies and strategies from six world regions—A Project Atlas® report* (pp. 49-54). New York: Institute of International Education.

China wants to have half a million international students in 10 years. (September 28, 2010). *The Chronicle of Higher Education*. Retrieved March 8, 2011, from http://chronicle.com/blogs/global/china-wants-to-have-half-a-million-international-students-in-10-years/27251

Chow, P. & Bhandari, R. (2010). *Open doors 2010: Report on international educational exchange*. New York: Institute of International Education.

Citizenship and Immigration Canada. (2010). *Facts and figures 2009: Immigration overview*. Retrieved February 21, 2011, from www.cic.gc.ca

"Erasmus Programme" (n.d.) Erasmusu. Retrieved March 21, 2011 from http://www.erasmusu.com/en/erasmus-programme

Fundación Universidad.es (2011). Spain. In R. Bhandari, R. Belyavina, & R. Gutierrez (Eds.), *Student mobility and the internationalization of higher education: National policies and strategies from six world regions—A Project Atlas® report* (pp. 97-100). New York: Institute of International Education.

German Academic Exchange Service (DAAD) (2011). Germany. In R. Bhandari, R. Belyavina, & R. Gutierrez (Eds.), *Student mobility and the internationalization of higher education: National policies and strategies from six world regions—A Project Atlas® report* (pp. 79-84). New York: Institute of International Education.

Hanbury-Tenison, M. (2010, November 7). Making the China connection. *Financial Times*.

Institute of International Education (IIE) (2011). United States. In R. Bhandari, R. Belyavina, & R. Gutierrez (Eds.), *Student mobility and the internationalization of higher education: National policies and strategies from six world regions—A Project Atlas® report* (pp. 37-44). New York: Institute of International Education.

International Education of South Africa (IEASA) (2011). South Africa. In R. Bhandari, R. Belyavina, & R. Gutierrez (Eds.), *Student mobility and the internationalization of higher education: National policies and strategies from six world regions—A Project Atlas® report* (pp. 15-20). New York: Institute of International Education.

Japan opts to "restructure" key university internationalization project. (November 19, 2010). *The Chronicle of Higher Education*. Retrieved March 8, 2011, from http://chronicle.com/blogs/global/japan-opts-to-restructure-key-university-internationalization-project/28091

Japan Student Services Organization (JASSO) (2011). Japan. In R. Bhandari, R. Belyavina, & R. Gutierrez (Eds.), *Student mobility and the internationalization of higher education: National policies and strategies from six world regions—A Project Atlas® report* (pp. 61-66). New York: Institute of International Education.

Kim, T. & Locke, W. (2010). *Transnational academic mobility and the academic profession*. London: Centre for Higher Education Research and Information, the Open University.

Kremmer, Janaki (2010, October 13). Australian conference focuses on drop in foreign students. *The Chronicle of Higher Education*. Retrieved March 4, 2011, from http://chronicle.com/article/Australian-Conference-Focuses/124908/

Kremmer, Janaki (2010, October 15). Educators say educators must do more to slow drop in international students. *The Chronicle of Higher Education*. Retrieved March 4, 2011, from http://chronicle.com/article/Educators-Say-Australian/124994/

Kubler, J. & Lennon, M. C. (2008). *International trade in higher education: Implications for the Commonwealth*. London: The Association of Commonwealth Universities.

Ly, Phuong (2008, May 15). Korea: The early study abroad trend. *Diverse: Issues in Higher Education 25*(7). Retrieved February 21, 2011 from http://diverseeducation.com/article/11150

Melcher, T. (2010, September). How Chinese families select overseas universities. *World Education News and Reviews, 23*(7). Retrieved February 21, 2011, from http://www.wes.org/ewenr/10sept/feature.htm

National Association of Universities and Higher Education Institutions (ANUIES). (2011). Mexico. In R. Bhandari, R. Belyavina, & R. Gutierrez (Eds.). *Student mobility and the internationalization of higher education: National policies and strategies from six world regions—A Project Atlas® report* (pp. 31-36). New York: Institute of International Education.

Netherlands Organization for International Cooperation in Higher Education (NUFFIC) (2011). Netherlands. In R. Bhandari, R. Belyavina, & R. Gutierrez (Eds.), *Student mobility and the internationalization of higher education: National policies and strategies from six world regions—A Project Atlas® report* (pp. 91-96). New York: Institute of International Education.

New Zealand Ministry of Education (2011). New Zealand. In R. Bhandari, R. Belyavina, & R. Gutierrez (Eds.), *Student mobility and the internationalization of higher education: National policies and strategies from six world regions—A Project Atlas® report* (pp. 119-122). New York: Institute of International Education.

OECD. (2010). *Education at a glance: OECD indicators 2010.* Paris: OECD.

OECD. (2011). *Reviews of national policies for Education: Kyrgyz Republic 2010: Lessons from PISA.* Paris: OECD.

Orazdurdy. (2009, August 13). Turkmen Ministry of Education to students: "You're traitors." Message posted to www.neweurasia.net

Orr, D., Schnitzer, K., & Frackmann, E. (2008). *Social and economic conditions of student life in Europe: Synopsis of indicators | Final report | Eurostudent III 2005–2008.* Germany: W. Bertelsmann Verlag.

Oz immigration dept. warns students' backlash on new reforms. (January 5, 2011). *The Economic Times.* Retrieved March 4, 2011, from http://articles.economictimes.indiatimes.com/2011-01-05/news/28425321_1_student-visas-permanent-residence-overseas-students

Partridge, Matthew. (2010, December 23). Mixed Reception. *The Times Higher Education* 23.

Rauhvargers, A., Deane, C. & Pauwels, W. (2009). *Bologna process stocktaking report 2009: Report from working groups appointed by the Bologna follow-up group to the ministerial conference in Leuven/Louvain-la-Neuve.* Retrieved from www.ond.vlaanderen.be/hogeronderwijs/bologna.

A third of foreign students stay on, minister says. (February 17, 2011). Voxy.co.nz. Retrieved on March 4, 2011, from http://www.voxy.co.nz/politics/third-foreign-students-stay-minister-says/5/8229

UNESCO Institute for Statistics. (2009). *Global education digest 2009: Comparing education statistics across the world.* Montreal: UNESCO-UIS.

UNESCO Institute for Statistics (2010). *Global education digest 2010: Comparing education statistics across the world.* Montreal: UNESCO-UIS.

Universities UK. (2007). *Policy briefing: Talent wars: The international market for academic staff.* London: Universities UK.

UK Border Agency. (2010). *The student immigration system: A consultation.* London: UK Border Agency Immigration Group. Retrieved from www.ukba.homeoffice.gov

World Education Services. (2010, 2011). *World Education News and Reviews, 23*(6–10). New York: WES. www.wes.org

ABOUT THE AUTHORS

Caroline Macready has been an education consultant since 2006 with her own company, Caroline Macready Consulting Ltd, advising on education at all levels, within the UK and internationally. She has worked on several education projects for OECD and the World Bank, including published reviews of Higher Education in Kazakhstan and Tertiary Education in Chile, for which she was Rapporteur; an international seminar on school improvement in Brasilia; and forthcoming reports on competitiveness and human capital development in Central Asia and Eastern Europe.

From 1995 to 2006, Caroline was a Deputy Director in England's Department for Education and Employment, which became the Department for Education and Skills. In the Education Department, Caroline was responsible for higher education quality, standards, access, governance and international issues, and for improving school performance and accountability. International work included advising Education Ministers in Estonia, Malta, Russia, and the U.S. Prior to 1995 Caroline worked in other Government Departments, including the Employment Department and the Home Office, where she headed the Division responsible for international legal co-operation against serious and organized crime. She has a Master of Arts degree in Politics, Philosophy & Economics from Oxford University.

Clive Tucker was the International Director of both the UK Department of Education and Skills and the UK Department for Work and Pensions until 2006. In that capacity he was responsible for the international aspects of UK policies on education and employment, including relations with the European Union, OECD, the G8 and the UN (particularly UNESCO and the ILO); the UK Government's programs to promote education exports by attracting international students to study in the UK and encouraging British universities and colleges to establish partnerships with institutions in other countries; establishing programs of bilateral educational cooperation with the governments of China, India, and other countries; and the UK's international educational exchange programs for teachers and students.

Clive was Chairman of the Employment Committee of the European Union from 2001 to 2003, and a member of the UK Fulbright Commission from 1998 until 2006. Since 2006 he has worked as an international education consultant advising a wide range of organizations. He is an Associate Director of the UK Specialist Schools and Academies Trust. Clive has a degree in History from Oxford University.

IIE Information and Resources

OPEN DOORS REPORT ON INTERNATIONAL EDUCATIONAL EXCHANGE

The *Open Doors Report on International Educational Exchange*, supported by the U.S. Department of State, Bureau of Educational and Cultural Affairs, provides an annual, comprehensive statistical analysis of academic mobility between the United States and other nations, and trend data over 60 years.

WEBSITE: www.iie.org/opendoors

THE CENTER FOR INTERNATIONAL PARTNERSHIPS IN HIGHER EDUCATION

The IIE Center for International Partnerships in Higher Education assists colleges and universities in developing and sustaining institutional partnerships with their counterparts around the world. A major initiative of the Center is the International Academic Partnerships Program, funded by the U.S. Department of Education's Fund for the Improvement of Postsecondary Education (FIPSE).

WEBSITE: www.iie.org/cip

ATLAS OF STUDENT MOBILITY

Project Atlas tracks migration trends of the millions of students who pursue education outside of their home countries each year. Data are collected on global student mobility patterns, country of origin, as well as leading host destinations for higher education.

WEBSITE: www.iie.org/projectatlas

IIE STUDY ABROAD WHITE PAPER SERIES: MEETING AMERICA'S GLOBAL EDUCATION CHALLENGE

An IIE policy research initiative that addresses the issue of increasing capacity in the U.S. and abroad, in order to help pave the way for substantial study abroad growth.

- Expanding Study Abroad Capacity at U.S. Colleges and Universities (May 2009)
- Promoting Study Abroad in Science and Technology Fields (March 2009)
- Expanding U.S. Study Abroad in the Arab World: Challenges & Opportunities (February 2009)
- Expanding Education Abroad at Community Colleges (September 2008)
- Exploring Host Country Capacity for Increasing U.S. Study Abroad (May 2008)
- Current Trends in U.S. Study Abroad & the Impact of Strategic Diversity Initiatives (May 2007)

WEBSITE: www.iie.org/StudyAbroadCapacity

IIE/AIFS FOUNDATION GLOBAL EDUCATION RESEARCH REPORTS

This series explores the most pressing and under-researched issues affecting international education policy today.

- Innovation through Education: Building the Knowledge Economy in the Middle East (August 2010)
- International India: A Turning Point in Educational Exchange with the U.S. (January 2010)
- Higher Education on the Move: New Developments in Global Mobility (April 2009)
- U.S.-China Educational Exchange: Perspectives on a Growing Partnership (October 2008)

IIE BRIEFING PAPERS

IIE Briefing Papers are a rapid response to the changing landscape of international education, offering timely snapshots of critical issues in the field.

- International Education as an Institutional Priority: What Every College and University Trustee Should Know (2011)
- The Value of International Education to U.S. Business and Industry Leaders: Key Findings from a Survey of CEOs (October 2009)
- The Three-year Bologna-compliant Degree: Responses from U.S. Graduate Schools (April 2009)
- Educational Exchange between the United States and China (July 2008)

WEBSITE: www.iie.org/research-and-publications

WEB RESOURCES

IIEPASSPORT.ORG
This free online search engine lists over 9,000 study abroad programs worldwide and provides advisers with hands-on tools to counsel students and promote study abroad.
WEBSITE: www.iiepassport.org

STUDY ABROAD FUNDING
This valuable funding resource helps U.S. students find funding for their study abroad.
WEBSITE: www.studyabroadfunding.org

FUNDING FOR UNITED STATES STUDY
This directory offers the most relevant data on hundreds of fellowships, grants, paid internships, and scholarships for study in the U.S.
WEBSITE: www.fundingusstudy.org

INTENSIVE ENGLISH USA
Comprehensive reference with over 500 accredited English language programs in the U.S.
WEBSITE: www.intensiveenglishusa.org

IIE RESOURCES FOR STUDY ABROAD
IIE offers a single point of entry to access valuable study abroad information, including policy research, data on study abroad trends, news coverage of new developments, fact sheets for students, and dates and deadlines for major scholarship and fellowship programs.
WEBSITE: www.iie.org/studyabroad

INTERNATIONALIZING THE CAMPUS
IIE administers a wealth of programs and provides a variety of services and resources to help U.S. colleges and universities develop and implement their strategies for greater campus internationalization.
WEBSITE: www.iie.org/internationalizing

FULBRIGHT PROGRAMS FOR U.S. STUDENTS
The Fulbright U.S. Student Program equips future American leaders with the skills they need to thrive in an increasingly global environment by providing funding for one academic year of study or research abroad, to be conducted after graduation from an accredited university.
SPONSOR: U.S. Department of State, Bureau of Educational and Cultural Affairs
WEBSITE: http://us.fulbrightonline.org

FULBRIGHT PROGRAMS FOR U.S. SCHOLARS
The traditional Fulbright Scholar Program sends 800 U.S. faculty and professionals abroad each year. Grantees lecture and conduct research in a wide variety of academic and professional fields.
SPONSOR: U.S. Department of State, Bureau of Educational and Cultural Affairs
WEBSITE: www.cies.org

Programs of the AIFS Foundation

The AIFS Foundation

The mission of the AIFS Foundation is to provide educational and cultural exchange opportunities to foster greater understanding among the people of the world. It seeks to fulfill this mission by organizing high quality educational opportunities for students, and providing grants to individuals and schools for participation in culturally enriching educational programs.

WEBSITE: www.aifsfoundation.org

ACADEMIC YEAR IN AMERICA

Each year, AYA brings nearly 1,000 high school students from around the world to the United States. They come for the school year, to live with American families and attend local high schools, learning about American culture and sharing their own languages and customs with their host families.

WEBSITE: www.academicyear.org

FUTURE LEADERS EXCHANGE PROGRAM (FLEX)

Established in 1992 under the FREEDOM Support Act and administered by the U.S. Department of State's Bureau of Educational and Cultural Affairs, FLEX encourages long-lasting peace and mutual understanding between the U.S. and countries of Eurasia.

YOUTH EXCHANGE AND STUDY PROGRAM (YES)

Since 2002, this U.S. Department of State high school exchange program has enabled students from predominantly Muslim countries to learn about American society and values, acquire leadership skills, and help educate Americans about their countries and cultures.

Programs of the American Institute for Foreign Study

American Institute For Foreign Study

The AIFS mission is to enrich the lives of young people throughout the world by providing them with educational and cultural exchange programs of the highest possible quality.

WEBSITE: www.aifs.com

AIFS COLLEGE STUDY ABROAD

AIFS is a leading provider of study abroad programs for college students. Students can study abroad for a summer, semester or academic year in 17 countries around the world.
WEBSITE: www.aifsabroad.com

AMERICAN COUNCIL FOR INTERNATIONAL STUDIES (ACIS)

For more than 30 years, ACIS has helped students and their teachers discover the world through premier travel and education. Teachers can choose destinations throughout Europe, the Americas and Asia.
WEBSITE: www.acis.com

AU PAIR IN AMERICA

Au Pair in America makes it possible for nearly 4,000 eager and skilled young adults from around the world to join American families and help care for their children during a mutually rewarding, year-long cultural exchange experience.
WEBSITE: www.aupairinamerica.com

CAMP AMERICA AND RESORT AMERICA

Each summer, Camp America and Resort America bring nearly 6,000 young people from around the world to the U.S. to work as camp counselors and resort staff.
WEBSITE: www.campamerica.aifs.com

SUMMER INSTITUTE FOR THE GIFTED (SIG)

SIG is a three-week academic, recreational and social summer program for gifted and talented students. Students from around the world in grades 4 through 11 can participate in SIG Residential programs offered at university campuses across the country including Dartmouth College, Princeton University, Yale University, UC Berkeley, UCLA, Amherst College, Emory University, Bryn Mawr College, Vassar College and University of Texas at Austin.
WEBSITE: www.giftedstudy.org

CULTURAL INSURANCE SERVICES INTERNATIONAL (CISI)

CISI is the leading provider of study abroad and international student insurance coverage. Since 1992, CISI has insured over 1 million international students and cultural exchange participants worldwide.

WEBSITE: www.culturalinsurance.com

AIFS Information & Resources

The following resources are available for download at:
www.aifsabroad.com/advisors/publications.asp

Diversity in International Education Summary Report

The Gender Gap in Post Secondary Study Abroad: Understanding and Marketing to Male Students

Study Abroad: A 21st Century Perspective, Vol I

Study Abroad: A 21st Century Perspective, Vol II: The Changing Landscape

Innocents at Home Redux – The Continuing Challenge to America's Future

Impact on Education Abroad on Career Development, Vol I

Impact on Education Abroad on Career Development: Four Community College Case Studies, Vol II